1 MONTH OF
FREE
READING

at

www.ForgottenBooks.com

By purchasing this book you are
eligible for one month membership to
ForgottenBooks.com, giving you
unlimited access to our entire
collection of over 1,000,000 titles via
our web site and mobile apps.

To claim your free month visit:
www.forgottenbooks.com/free897362

ISBN 978-0-266-84033-6
PIBN 10897362

THE STUDENTS' HISTORY

OF

RAJPOOTANA,

Being an account of The Princes of Rajpootana
From the earlist ages To the
modern times,   .

BY

AMRITA LAL DE, B. A., B. L.,

PROFESSOR OF HISTORY,

MAHARAJA'S COLLEGE,

JEYPORE,

RAJPOOTANA,

AND

Author of "The Flowers of India,"
"Kissa Shan Eli," the "Yoga
System," "Essay on Cow-
slaughter," &c. &c,.

CALCUTTA.

PRINTED BY

BAMA CHUBAN DUTTA, AT THE NOBO SARASSUTA PRESS,
84, RAJA RAJBULLUV'S STREET, BUGBAZAR.
1889.

THE

ANNALS OF THE STATES OF RAJ-POOTANA.

"It is only by attracting attention to the prominent features in Rajpootana history, by casting light upon the salient features of the career of the Princes of Rajpootana and making them stand out boldly from the canvas, that it will ever be possible to interest the general reader in Indian affairs."

"Times" *altered*.

TO

Colonel C. K. M. WALTER,

Agent,

GOVERNOR-GENERAL,

RAJPOOTANA,

THIS WORK

WRITTEN

IN THE PROVINCE,

OF WHICH

He may be regarded as the best

organizer and wellwisher,

IS,

BY PERMISSION,

Most respectfully *Inscribed* By his humble servant,

The *Author.*

PREFACE.

There are some histories of Rajpootana now before the Public, but they are bulky in size, voluminous, difficult of understanding, and not suitable to serve as a stepping-stone for the youths of Rajpootana to the learning of the history of the Rajpoot States. But a hand-book of the History of Rajpootana likely to prove interesting and useful to the Indian students, and especially to the youths of Rajpootana, and be easily comprehended by them, is not yet in existence.

Such a concise and plain history in *English* is a *desideratum* and has been long felt as such.

The boys in the schools of Rajpootana know well the facts and events narrated in the histories of England, Greece and Rome, but an account of their own native land, *Rajpootana*, they are almost, if not wholly, ignorant of.

To supply this want, the present *Students' History of Rajpootana* is published and is meant to be used as a *text-book* in history in the higher classes of the Junior Department of the schools in Rajpootana.

I know not how this little unpretending volume will be received by the Public at large; but if the Educational Authorities in the different States of Rajpootana consider it fit to be introduced as a *text-book* in history in the Second and Third Junior classes of the Schools under their control and management, I shall deem my labor well repaid.

The work before the Public must necessarily be of the nature of a compilation. I have gone to the best authorities on the subject and taken much from them. The books I have consulted, and upon which I have based this

little volume, are "The Rajpootana Gazetteer," Colonel
Tod's "Annals and Antiquities of Rajasthan," and Colonel
G. B. Malleson's "The Native States of Rajpootana."

All the Native States treated in this book, except
Ajmere-Marwara, which is itself a British territory, are
in subsidiary alliance with the British Government.

One word as to the mode of division I have adopted
in this volume. I have thought it convenient, instead of
grouping the States according to the natural order of the
divisions in which they lie, to follow the order of their
individual size. I have indicated the history of the several
States in Rajpootana in a plain language and in an easy
style best adapted to the juvenile capacities of the students
for whom it is intended, and with such detail as a mere
sketch of them authorizes. The *work* presents a brief and
simple outline of the History of Rajpootana from a very
early age to the latest date. It is a history which every
youth in Rajpootana, if not in India, ought to be familiar
with; and the author would fain hope that the interest
shown to the subject will be some compensation for the
mode in which it has been treated.

With reference to dates of events, or the birth, accession or death of any of the ruling chiefs of any of the
States of Rajpootana, about which the authorities I have
consulted did not agree, I have thought it proper to adopt
that which has stood comparison with those fixed by
distinguished historians of the Indian Empire of Her
Gracious Majesty the Queen-Empress.

89, D. C. Mitter's
Street, Calcutta.   }   AMRITA LAL DE.
May 1st,
.1889.

TABLE OF CONTENTS.

PART I.
THE GEOGRAPHY OF RAJPOOTANA.

PART II.

THE HISTORY OF RAJPOOTANA.

THE
STUDENTS' HISTORY
OF
RAJPOOTANA.

————◇————

INTRODUCTION.

India has undergone various stages of its political history, which furnish useful subjects of study to the historian and the statesman. The first stage was a peaceful period when the Indian nation was governed by its own Maharajas. This period was certainly the best portion of its history for the study of the character and the institutions of the people. In ancient times the land of the Rajpoots was the seat of glory, heroism, honesty and chastity. Among the records of the Rajpoot princes are to be found *deeds* which undoubtedly reflect glory and renown to the actors and to the land they dwelt upon,—*deeds* of men and women, of princes and princesses, of heroes and heroines, proving without a shadow of doubt that they belonged to the most chivalrous race that ever lived upon the surface of this habitable world,—*deeds* which clearly show that they knew not double dealing in their transactions with others or faithlessness to the family-bond with which they were bound for life.

The history of such a country is really a mine of jewels

and gold which historians cannot but be glad to open to the benefit of the general reader.

The second stage of Indian history commences with the invasion of India by Mahmud of Ghazni about the beginning of the eleventh century after Christ. The Mahomedan period was followed by that of the Mogul supremacy with the conquest of India by Babar in 1526, forming the third period of Indian history. The fourth stage of Indian history dawns with the downfall of the Mogul Empire and the rise of the Mahrattas upon its ruin. And the fifth stage begins from the breaking down of the Mahratta confederacy and the commencement of the sovereignty of the British power in India.

During all these revolutions in government, Rajpootana underwent corresponding changes in its *regime* and condition, and in the formation, growth and development of the several states of which it is made up, a sketch of the history of which is given in their proper places in the following pages.

This book has been divided into two parts with sub-divisions of each. The history of a country can be read with advantage and accuracy when its geography is thoroughly known. The *first* part of the book, therefore, has been devoted to the geography of Rajpootana and the *second* part gives a short and plain account of Rajpootana itself and a cursory narrative of each of the eighteen Native States and the British territory Ajmere-Marwara, of which it is made up, from the earliest period down to the latest date. But the narrative shows "little of the action of the people, but like the history of all governments of the past, consists simply of the wars, the exploits and succession of their rulers. But it is by no means wanting in events of interest, or in indications of life and vitality calculated in many instances to excite the pride of the rulers and the ruled of these states in their past. And pride in the past, I need hardly say, affords the best guarantee for development and improvement in the future."

In the portion of this book treating of the geography of Rajpootana, I have not only dealt with a general outline of the country of Rajpootana and of the several states of which it is composed ; but I have treated, in as concise a manner as possible, of the staff of life, of tribes and castes, of religion, of industrial occupations, of manners and customs, and of government, that existed and now exist in Rajpootana.

In the historical portion of the book, therefore, a succinct narrative of facts and events, that took place in Rajpootana, has been attempted, and no mention is made of the condition, or manners and customs, or the government of the people of Rajasthan.

PART I.

THE

GEOGRAPHY

OF

RAJPOOTANA.

CHAPTER I.

GENERAL DESCRIPTION.

Rajpootana is situated to the east of Sindh and south of the Punjab, and is rather greater than the Bombay Presidency. It is so called from the Rajpoots being the ruling class. The word Rajpootana signifies a territorial circle which contains nineteen states including the British district of Ajmere-Marwara in the centre. It lies between the parallels of 23° and 30° north latitude, and 69° 30´ and 78° 15´ east longitude. Its area is about 130,934 square miles and population about ten millions. It is bounded on the west by Sindh, on the south-west by Bhawalpur, on the south and south-east by the dominions of Sindia, Holkar and Gaekwar, and on the north by the Punjab and north-east by the North-West Provinces.

It may be divided into five groups of States,—

I. The States of Jeysulmere, Marwar or Jodhpur and Bikaneer, in the west and north.

II. Ulwur, and Shekhawati in Jeypore, in the north-east.

III. Jeypore, Bharatpur, Dholpur, Karauli, Bundi, Kotah and Jhalawar, in the east and south.

IV. Partapgarh, Banswara, Dungarpur, Meywar or Oodeypore and Sirohee and Abu, in the south-west.

V. The British district of Ajmere, Kishengarh and Tonk in the centre.

Rajpootana is naturally · divided into two principal divisions by the Aravalli hills, namely,—

I. Rajpootana north-west of the Aravalli range including the Great Indian Desert, and

II. Rajpootana south-east of the range.

The character of the first natural division of Rajpootana is *arid*, sandy, unproductive and ill-watered, improving from a mere desert in the far west and north-west to a comparatively habitable and fertile lands towards the north-east. Along the whole of this north-west division, the Aravalli ranges represent a coast-line, partly fenced by high cliffs and partly by an irregular shore pierced by bays and inlets against which the sea of sands flows up continually from the shelving plains of the west. The second division, Rajpootana south-east of the Aravalli hills, contains the higher and more fertile districts that stretch inland behind the coast-line represented by them. In contrast to the sandy plains which are the uniform feature, more or less modified, of the north-west division of Rajpootana, this south-eastern division contains hill-ranges and wood-lands, wide vales, fertile table-lands and excellent soil, and is traversed by considerable rivers.

CHAPTER II.

MOUNTAINS. HILLS. MINERALS.

Mountains.—Of mountains and hills the Aravallis are by far the most important. It has been already stated that the Aravalli hills mark off the whole of Rajpootana into two natural divisions. Their elevated masses influence the climate of Rajpootana, collecting the waters and directing the outfall of all the western rivers. One of the most conspicuous peaks overlooking the city, Ajmere, is that on which stands the famous fort of Taragarh. Mount Abu belongs by position to the Aravalli range. It is a cluster of hills with the highest peak rising to 5,653 feet above the level of the sea, standing away about seven miles from the western face of the Aravalli range. The Aravalli mountains running north-east from mount Abu, may be taken as the boundary of the desert, and, geographically, as the extreme northwest of the Deccan plateau. The general character of the Aravallis is its primitive formation. Granite reposing on variety of angle on massive, compact, dark-blue slate, almost keeps it concealed. The internal valleys abound in quartz and slate of every hue, which gives a most singular appearance to the roofs of the houses and temples when the sun shines upon them. The Aravalli and its subordinate hills are rich both in mineral and metallic products.

Besides gold, silver. copper, lead and tin, this chain contains rock crystal, amathysts, chrysoline carbuncles and garnets, as well as a few emeralds.

The highest peak of this chain, Mount Abu, is the seat of the Agent, Governor-General, Rajpootana. In 1845, the Rao of Sirohee made over to the British Government some lands on Mount Abu for the establishment of a sanitarium.

Hills.—Of the hill ranges of Rajpootana the chief are the hills of Jeypore and Ulwur, the heights of Biana and Alipur in Bharatpur, the Bundi hills, and the Makundara range near Kota.

Minerals.—The following minerals are obtained in Rajpootana. Copper is found in Khetri, in Shekhawati in Jeypore, and in Ulwur, and in small quantities in Jeypore, Ajmere and Sirohee. Lead is obtained in Taragarh hills near Ajmere, near Gudha in Jeypore, and in Jodhpur. Zinc is found in Jawar in Oodeypore and at Sojat in Jodhpur. Cobalt is obtained in Khetri. Iron is found in Bhaogarh and Rajgarh in Ulwur, in Ajmere, in the Biana hills in Bharatpur, in the Bundi hills, and in Jodhpur and Kotah. Alum and blue vitriol (sulphate of copper) are manufactured at Khetri. Slates are found in the Ajabgarh group of the Ulwur hills.

Limestones are abundantly obtained in Ulwur, Bundi and Jeysulmere. Two forms of limestones found in Rajpootana stand pre-eminent among the ornamental stones of India for their beauty. The first of these are the Raialo limestones of the Ulwur group of rocks and at Mukrana in Jodhpur, employed in building the Taj Mahal at Agra. The second are the limestones of Jeysulmere. Sandstones are found in Bharatpur and in Jodhpur.

The salt-sources for which Rajpootana is celebrated, are the following lakes in it, namely,—Sambhar on the

borders of Jeypore and Jodhpur yielding about thirty
lacs of maunds of salt per year, Kachor Rewassa in
Shekhawati yielding one and a half lac of maunds per
year, Didwana and Phalodi in Jodhpur yielding four lacs
and one and a half lac per year respectively, Chapur in
Bikaneer, Pokharan in Jodhpur, and Kanod in Jeysulmere.
Beds of rivers in Rajpootana, such as *Loni*, supply also
large quantities of salt.

CHAPTER III.

CLIMATE. HYGIENE. FORESTS. THE STAFF OF LIFE. RIVERS. LAKES.

Climate.—The rainfall is very unequally distributed in
Rajpootana. The western side may be called the rainless
district. In the south-west of it the fall is copious, and
at Abu it sometimes passes one hundred inches. Along the
southern states, the land gets rain from the Indian Ocean
and from the Bay of Bengal. The northern part of Rajpootana gets a scanty share of the wintry rains of Northern
India, and the southern part gets almost none at all.

In summer the sun's heat is much the same all over the
country ; and, except in the high hills, it is great every
where. Hot winds and dust storms are known more or less
through-out ; but in the sandy half-desert tracts of the
north, they are as violent as in any part of India, while in
the southerly parts they are tempered by hills, verdure
and water.

In winter the climate of the north is much colder than
in lower districts with hard frost and ice upon the Bikaneer borders ; and from great dryness of the atmosphere

in these inland countries, the change of temperature between day and night is sudden, excessive and very trying.

Hygiene.—The climatic conditions of Rajpootana influe-
ence, as they do every-where, the general health of the
people. The epidemic diseases are of a malarious type.
Cholera visitations occur in the Eastern States, the Western
States being free from them on account of the sparsely
populated and semi-desert nature of these districts over
which the winds travel freely. The condition of the water-
supply and the comparative poorness of the grain, *bajra*,
which forms the staple food of the people in the north-west,
give rise to dyspeptic maladies and to skin-diseases. Northern Rajpootana is periodically desolated by famine and
death caused by failure of rainfall. But notwithstanding
its drawbacks, Rajpootana may be generally reckoned as
one of the healthiest countries in India, at least for the na-
tives of the place.

Forests.—Mount Abu is well-wooded from summit to
skirts and possesses several value-able kinds of timber. In
Sirohee and all over the south-western Meywar, the wood-
lands stretch for many miles. In Bharatpur there are some
value-able woodlands.

Trees.—Of the trees in Rajpootana the most prominent
are the peepul, the banyan, the *ungur*, the mulberry, the ta-
marind, the mangoe, the *nim*, the *babul*, the *ber*, the *siris*,
the *jamun*, the pomegranate, and the peach.

The Staff of Life.—Wheat, barley, millet, *bajra*, oat,
jowar, maize, sugar-cane, water-melons and rice, form the
chief staff of life.

Animals.—Rajpootana is the breeding ground of some of
the finest races of cattle, horses, camels and bullocks in
India. Nagor is famous for bullocks, Mallani for horses,

and Bikaneer for camels. Generally speaking the country of Rajpootana is barren and infertile.

Rivers.—In the north-west division of Rajpootana the only river of any consequence is the *Loni*, which rises in the Pushkar valley close to Ajmere, and runs south-west for about two hundred miles and falls into the Runn of Cutch. A small stream in the north of Jeypore, *Nala*, flows northward for some distance and there is lost in the sands of the Shekhawati country. The *Chambal* is by far the largest river in Rajpootana. It rises upwards of 2000 feet above the sea near the summits of the Vindhya mountains, and runs in a northern direction through Malwa till it enters Rajpootana at Chaurasgarh on the south-west border of Meywar, and meets the Brahmani river at Bhaneswargarh, then flows north-east to Kotah city, and passing along the whole length of the Karauli state, flows by Dholepur and falls into Jumna. Its length is 560 miles. The next river is *Banas* which rises in Meywar and falls into the *Chambal* near the Bundi state. The Western *Banas* and *Shubarnamati* take their rise from the hills of Meywar, and, after passing Rajpootana, flow towards the south-west. The river *Mahi* waters the territories of Partapgarh and Banswara, and one of its chief tributaries, the Som, flows through Meywar.

Lakes.—There are no natural fresh water lakes in Rajpootana, the only considerable lake being the well-known salt lake at Sambhar. The finest artificial lakes are within the territory of the Oodeypore State, namely,—*Debar, Kangraoli, Oodeysagar* and *Pechola*.

There are some smaller lakes or tanks in Meywar, but they are of very little importance.

CHAPTER IV.

TRIBES AND CASTES. FORTRESSES. RELIGION. INDUSTRIAL OCCUPATIONS. MANNERS AND CUSTOMS.

Tribes and *Castes.*—The people of Rajpootana are made up of the *Charuns* or *Bhats*, the *Rajpoots*, the *Jains*, the *Jats*, the *Goozars*, the *Minas*, the *Mers*, the *Bhils*, the *Meos*, and the *Brahmins*, the *Kayeths* and the *Banyas.*

Fortresses.—There are many strong and beautiful fortresses in Rajpootana, namely,—*Taragarh* above Ajmere, *Chitore, Kamalmir, Mandulgarh* and *Indergarh* among the hills about *Banas* and *Chambal,* the *Jodhpur* fortress, *Nargarh* and *Amber* fortresses in Jeypore, *Gugron* in Jhalrapatan, and *Runthambor* at the confluence of the *Banas* and *Chambal.*

Religion.—The vast majority of the people of Rajpootana are *Hindus* with a very strong infusion of the *Jaina* sect. There are also the *Mussulman* sects, the *Dadu Punthis* and the *Ram Such* sect. Besides these there are some secret societies and mystic sects given to demon-worship and nameless *orgies.*

Industrial occupation.—The mass of the people is occupied in *agriculture.* In the large towns *banking* and *commerce* flourish. In the north the staple products for exports are *salt, gram, wool* and *cotton.* In the south the great articles of export are *opium* and *cotton.* The import consists of *sugar, hard-ware, piece-goods* and other miscellaneous articles not manufactured in Rajpootana.

Manners and *customs.*—The people of Rajpootana like the orthodox Hindus of other provinces in India are averse to sudden changes. They adhere strongly to the manners and customs, rites and ceremonies of their ancestors the Aryans of old. Infanticide and Sati rite which prevailed here before have been stopped by the intervention of the paramount British Power. They are still fond of marrying their infants and of early marriage, and do not marry their widows. They expend large sums of money in celebrating religious festivals, in marriages and *Shrads.* *Parda* system is almost unknown among the females of the middle and lower classes of people of Rajpootana. The women here are very fond of putting on many-coloured dresses and gold, silver and pearl ornaments, and delight in singing all sorts of song on all occasions and at all places.

CHAPTER V.

THE RAJPOOTANA STATES. THEIR BOUNDARIES, EXTENT, AREA, POPULATION, CHIEF TOWNS AND THEIR GOVERNMENT.

There are, as I have stated before, five groups of states in Rajpootana.

I. The States of *Jeysulmere, Marwar* or *Jodhpur* and *Bikaneer*, in the west and north.

Jeysulmere.—The state of *Jeysulmere* is bounded on the north by Bharatpur, on the east by Bikaneer and Marwar, on the south by Marwar and on the west by Sindh.

Its area is 16,447 square miles, and its population is

about 72,000 souls, of whom 43,500 are Hindus, 26,000 Mussulmans, and 2,500 Jains.

Its chief towns are *Jeysulmere, Bap, Birsilpur* and *Bikrampur.*

Marwar or *Jodhpur.*—*Jodhpur* called also *Marwar* is the largest in extent of the Rajpootana States.

It is bounded on the north by Bikaneer and Shekhawati, on the east by Jeypore and Kishengarh, on the south by Sirohee and Palanpore, and on the west by the Runn of Cutch and Sindh.

It is 290 miles long and 130 miles broad. Its area is 37,000 square miles, and population is 2,000,000 souls, of whom 86 per. cent are Hindus, 10 per. cent Jains, and 4 per. cent Mussulmans.

The chief towns of it are *Jodhpur, Didwana, Mairta, Nagore, Mundor, Nadol, Peepur, Pali, Phallodi* and *Pokaran.*

Bikaneer.—The state of *Bikaneer* is bounded on the north by Bhawalpur and the Sirsa district, on the east by the Hissar district and Jeypore, on the south by Jodhpur, and on the west by Jeysulmere.

Its chief towns are *Bikaneer, Bideswar, Ampgarh, Bhatnir, Bahadron, Choru, Nohur, Rajgarh, Ranee, Rattangarh, Saratgarh and Sujangarh.*

II. The States of *Ulwur,* and *Shekhawati* (a district subject to and included in the state of Jeypore) are in the north-east.

Ulwur.—The state of *Ulwur* is bounded on the north by Gargaon, Nabha and Kot-Kasim, on the east by Bharatpur and Gargaon, on the south by Jeypore, and on the west by Jeypore, Kot Pootli, Nabha and Patiala.

It has an area of 3,024 square miles and its population is 778,596 souls, of whom 180,225 are Mussulmans and the rest, Hindus.

Its chief towns are *Ulwur, Tijara, Rajgarh, Luchmun-garh, Nimrani, Macheri* and *Ramgarh.*

Shekhawati.—It being a tract of land included in the state of Jeypore, need not be separately mentioned.

III.   The States of *Jeypore, Bharatpur, Dholpur, Karauli, Bundi, Kotah* and *Jhalawar.*

Jeypore.—The state of *Jeypore* including Shekhawati is bounded on the north by Bikaneer, Lohari, Jhagur and Patiala, on the south by Gwalior, Bundi, Tonk, Meywar, and Ajmere, on the east by Ulwur, Bharatpur and Karauli, and on the west by Kishengarh, Marwar and Bikaneer.

Its area is 14,465 square miles and population is 1,900,000 souls, the population of the city, Jeypore, being 137,887 souls.

Its chief towns are *Jeypore, Patan, Khandela, Amber, Chatsoo, Sanganeer, Sambhar, Rupgarh, Oniara, Ramgarh, Shikar, Luchmungarh, Fateypur, Bissan, Mandawa, Nawal-garh* and *Jhunjhnu.*

Bharatpur.—The state of Bharatpur is bounded on the north by Gargaon, on the east by Muttra and Agra, on the south by Dholpur, Karauli and Jeypore, and on the west by Jeypore, Ulwur and Gargaon.

Its length is 76 miles and breadth 63 miles.

Its area is 1974 square miles, and population, 743,710 souls, of whom 630,242 are Hindus and 113,445 are Mussulmans.

Its chief towns are *Bharatpur, Bhusawar, Beana, Balla-garh, Dig, Gopalgarh, Kama, Kanua, Kombhar, Papuri, Ruplas, Sikri* and Weir.

Dholpur.—The state of *Dholpur* is bounded on the north and east by the district of Agra, on the west by Bharatpur and Karauli, and on the south by the river Chambal. Its area is 1.174 square miles, and population, 227,976 souls, of whom 36 884 are Brahmins, 32.092 Chamars, 23,703 Thakoors, 17,229 Goozars, 15,090 Kachis, and 10,620 Minas.

Its chief towns are *Dholpur, Báree, Nagore, Mumsa* and *Rajakhera.*

Karauli.—The state of *Karauli* lies to the south of Bharatpur. It is bounded on the east by Dholpur, on the south by *Chambal,* on the north-east by Jeypore and on the west by *Banas.*

Its area is 1,878 square miles and population, 188,000 souls, consisting of Brahmins, Rajpoots, Traders, Goozars, Minas, Chamars, Kachis, Mussulmans and Koolis.

Its chief towns are *Karauli, Mandreh* and *Machilpur.*

Bundi.—The state of *Bundi* is bounded on the north by Jeypore and Tonk, on the south and east by Kotah and on the west by Meywar. Its area is 2,218 square miles and population is 224,000 souls.

Its chief towns are *Bundi, Indergarh, Dublona* and *Nainwah.*

Kotah.—The state of *Kotah* is bounded on the north and west by Bundi and on the south and east by the Central India Agency. Its area is about 5000 square miles and population about 527,000 souls.

Its chief towns are *Kotah, Burrod, Nahargarh, Rajgarh, Sangod* and *Sultanpur.*

Jhalawar.—The state of *Jhalawar* is bounded on the north by Kotah, on the south by Rajgarh and the dominions of Sindia and Holkar, and on the east and west by the dominions of Sindia and Holkar.

Its area is 2,500 square miles, and population, 226,000.

Its chief towns are *Jhalrapatan*, *Chaoni* and *Gazraun*.

IV.   The States of *Partapgarh*, *Banswara*, *Dungarpur*, *Meywar* or *Oodeypore* and *Sirohi*, are in the south-west.

Partapgarh.—The state of *Partapgarh* is bounded on the north-west by Meywar, on the south-east by Jaura and Piploda, on the north-east by Sindia's dominions and on the south-west and west by Banswara.

Its area is 1,450 square miles, and population is 150,000 souls, of whom the majority are Bhils.

Its chief towns are *Partapgarh* and *Deolia*.

Banswara.—The state of *Banswara* is bounded on the north and north-west by Dungarpur and Meywar, on the north-east by Partapgarh, on the south by the Central India Agency, and on the west by Rewah Kanta.

Its area is about 1,500 square miles and population, 150,000 souls.

Its chief towns are *Banswara*, *Karinjra* and *Kusalgarh*.

Dungarpur--—The state of *Dungarpur* is bounded on the north by Meywar, on the east by Meywar and the river Mahi, on the south by *Mahi* and on the west by Rewah and Mahi Kanta.

Its area is about 952 square miles, and population, 100,000 souls.

Its chief towns are *Dungarpur*, *Sagwara*, and *Galliakot*.

Meywar or *Oodeypore*.—The state of Meywar is bounded on the north by Ajmere and Marwara, on the west by the Aravalli mountains, on the south-west by Mahi Kanta, on the south by Dungarpur, Banswara and Partapgarh, and on the east by Bundi, Kotah and Sindia's dominions.

Its area is about 12,929 square miles and population is 1,161,400, consisting of Rajpoots, Meis, Bhils and Minas.

Its chief towns are *Oodeypore, Amlee, Banera, Bednor,
Bhinda, Chitor, Dubla, Deogarh, Goosur, Gangapoora, Jahaj-
pur, Kuraboor, Nathdwara, Reypore, Rajgarh, Rajnagar,
Rashma, Rohera, Sanganeer, Sawu* and *Salumbar.*

Sirohi.—The state of *Sirohi* is bounded on the north
by Marwar, on the south by Palanpur and the Mahi
Kanta state, on the east by Meywar and on the west by
Marwar.

Its area is 3000 square miles and population, 153,000
souls.

Its chief towns are *Sirohi, Abu* and *Erinpura.*

V.—The British district of *Ajmere-Marwara, Kishengarh*
and *Tonk,* are in the centre.

Ajmere.—The British district of *Ajmere* is bounded on
the north by Kishengarh and Marwar, on the south by
Marwara and Meywar, on the east by Kishengarh and
Jeypore and on the west by Marwar.

Its area is about 2,069 square miles and population,
309,914 souls.

Marwara.—The British district of *Marwara* is bounded
on the north by Marwar and Ajmere, on the south by
Meywar, on the east by Ajmere and Meywar, and on the
west by Marwar.

Its area is about 641 square miles and population,
86,417 souls.

Ajmere-Marwara.—The united district of *Ajmere-Marwara* has an area of 2,710·680 square miles and a population
of 396,331 souls.

Its chief towns are *Ajmere, Beawar, Kekri* and *Pushkor.*

Tonk.—The state of *Tonk* is bounded on the north,
east and west by the principality of Jeypore and on the
south by Bundi.

Its area is 1,688 square miles and population, 320,000 souls.

Its chief towns are *Tonk, Lawa, Nimbera* and *Rampura.*

Government.—The system of government which prevails among the Rajpoots is alike to *Feudalism* of ancient Europe. With them the founder of a state, after reserving a *Demesne* for himself, divided the rest of the country among his relations, according to the Hindu laws of partition.

The chief to whom each share was assigned, owed military service and general obedience to the prince, but exercised unlimited authority within his own lands. He, in his turn, divided his lands on similar terms among his relations, and a chain of vassal chiefs was thus established, to whom the civil government as well as the military force of the country was committed.

This plan differs from the *Feudal* system in Europe, as being founded on the principle of family partition, and not on that of securing the services of great military leaders. The origin of present possession in family claims is still alive in the memory of the Rajpoot chiefs, who view the prince as their *coparcener* in one point of view, though their sovereign in another. The rule of partition was adhered to after the conquest, and each chief in succession, was obliged to provide an *appanage* for the younger members of his father's family. When any of the claimants remained inadequately provided for, he was assisted to conquer and found new estates in other countries. The example of granting lands came gradually to be extended to strangers; and many fiefs are now held by Rajpoots of entirely distinct tribes. by chiefs of other castes and by Mussulmans.

The government is vested in the ruler of the estate, who is to manage his affairs with the assistance of his ministers and civil, criminal and military officials. He is to act in his own domains with justice, chastise foreign foes with rigour, behave sincerely to his friends, punish the offenders, protect the weak, the helpless and the good, and treat with lenity the Brahmins. He is to be honest, popular, dexterous in business, learned and good.

The Rajpoot princes and other chiefs of the States in Rajpootana govern their domains according to their own laws and customs, and possess various degrees of independence ; but are all supervised, and to a certain extent, controlled by the Agent, Governor-General, Rajpootana, and are advised, instructed and watched over by the Residents or Political Agents appointed by the paramount British Government to reside at their capitals.

They are in subsidiary alliance with, and under the protection of, the British Government, to which they pay annual tribute. They are bound by treaties not to fight with each other or declare war against any foreign foe without the express consent of the paramount power, and, in return of the British protection, they are bound to assist the British Government with men and money in times of danger, foreign attack or necessity. Thus constituted the several States of Rajpootana are day by day prospering, and free from troubles and disturbances that prevailed there in days gone by. Under the powerful and beneficent rule of the British Power, life and property are now secure every where in Rajpootana.

PART II.

THE

HISTORY

OF

RAJPOOTANA.

INTRODUCTORY CHAPTER.

The "Agni Pooran" says "when Ocean quitted his bounds and caused universal destruction by Brahma's command, *Manu*, fourth in descent from *Brahma* through *Marichi*, who dwelt near the Hymalaya mountains, was giving water to the Gods in the Kritarna river, when a fish fell into his hands. A voice commanded him to preserve it. The fish expanded into an enormous size. Manu with his sons and their wives and the sages, with the seed of every living being, entered into a vessel which was fastened to a horn on the head of the fish, and thus they were preserved."

In the *Bhavishya Pooran* again it is stated that *Vawaswata* (sun born) Manu ruled at the mountain *Sumaru*. Of his seed was Cacustha Raja who obtained sovereignty at *Ayodhya*, and his descendants filled and spread over the globe."

"Most nations have indulged the desire of fixing the source whence they issued, and few spots possess more interest than this elevated *Madhya Bhumi* or central region of Asia, where the *Amu, Oxus* or *Jehoon,* and other rivers have their rise, and in which both the *Surya* and *Indoo* races claim the hill *Sumaru*, sacred to a great patriarchal ancestor, whence they migrated eastward to the Indus and Ganges, and founded their first establishment in *Kosala*, the capital, *Ayodhya* or *Oudh.*"

From *Veda Byas* we learn that fifty-seven princes of the Solar line came between Manu and Ram, and fifty-eight princes of the 'Lunar race ruled over the same period. *Icshwacu*, son of Manu, was the founder of the kingdom of *Ayodhya* and a succession of fifty-seven princes occupied it from *Icshwacu* to Ram. *Boodha*, fifth in descent from Brahma through *Atri*, founded the Lunar line, and *Prayag* (Allahabad) their first capital, was founded by *Puru*, sixth in descent from *Boodha*. From the sons of *Yayati*, fifth in descent from *Bhooda*, the Lunar races descend in unequal lengths. The lines from *Yadu*, a son of *Yayati*, concluding with *Krishna* and his cousin *Kansa*, exhibit fifty-seven and fifty-nine descents from *Yayati* : while *Yudhisthera*, *Sal* and *Jarasandhu*, contemporaries of *Krishna* and *Kansa*, are fifty-one, forty-six and forty-seven generations, respectively, from the common ancestor *Yayati.*

From Ram through his sons. *Lava* and *Kush*, all the tribes termed " Suryavansa " or Race of the Sun, claim descent, as the present princes of Meywar, Jeypore, Marwar, Bikaneer and their numerous clans ; while from the Lunar (Indoo) line of *Boodha* and *Krishna*, the families of Jeysulmere and Cutch, extending throughout the Indian Desert, from the Sutlej to the Ocean, deduce their pedigrees.

The Rajpoots suppose that they were established in India about 2,000 years before Christ. But it is now nearly certain that their invasion of India dates from a much more recent epoch.

According to the Brahmans, the *Kshatriyas* were all destroyed by a general rising of the other castes, which was directed by *Parusarama,* an incarnation of *Vishnu,* several centuries before Christ, and we find several families of the *Soodras,* among others the *Mauriyas,* succeeded each other on the imperial throne of *Magadha.* The Rajpoots made their first appearance on the political stage of India about the sixth or seventh century. They had remained a long time established on the banks of the Indus, and had invaded, little by little, the western portions of India. Between the sixth and seventh centuries the Rajpoot tribes became all powerful. The *Chandelas* took possession of Malwa, the *Chohans* and *Rahtores* seized Kanauj and Delhi, and the *Ghelots* and *Baghelas* took Meywar and Gujrat. In the 11th century about the period of the first Mussulman inroad into the interior of Northern India, the leading Rajpoot tribes were the *Solankies* of *Anhalwara* ruling in Gujrat, the *Chohans* at Ajmere, the *Rahtors* at Kanauj, and the *Ghelots* in Meywar. The Great Desert between Sindh and Rajpootana sheltered the Rajpoot clans from any serious inroads of the Arabs, and therefore the first Mussulman invasions into India found the Rajpoot dynasties in all the chief cities of the North, and ruling large territories throughout the rich Gangetic plains—at Lahore, Delhi, Kanauj and *Ayodhya.*

Mahmud of Ghazni defeated the *Solankies* of Gujrat, but was barred by the *Chohans* of Ajmere. In 1170, a furious war took place between the *Chohans* and *Solankies* with fatal consequences. The internal quarrels weakened the Rajpoot dynasties and paved the way for their easy downfall, though the *Chohans* fought hard before they were driven out from Ajmere and Delhi.

The Mussulmans gradually over-awed the Rajpoot clans and pressed them back into the outlying districts which they have held up to the present day. The *Bhattis* settled in Jeysulmere in the extreme north-west, having been driven across the Sutlej by the Ghaznavi conquerors. The *Rahtores* settled down among the sands of Marwar; the *Sesodyas* pushed inward from north-east and south-west on the Meywar plains behind the Aravallis, and the *Jadavs* sheltered themselves along the Chambal. From these and other migrations grew up gradually the States now govern-ed by the Rajpoot chiefs ; the non-Rajpoot States being of a very different and much more recent formation. The larger States represent the acquisitions of the more power-ful and predominant clans ; and the smaller States are either the separate conquests of a sept that parted company from the main clan or the *Appanage* of some chief who set up independently. In this way the whole of Raj-pootana seems to have been portioned out among the tribes which we find there now ; and the territories which have been gradually added and strengthened by incessent feuds, are now called States, each under the rule of the chief of the dominant class.

The Rajpoots (sons of kings), the ruling race of Raj-pootana and from whom the country is so called, are tall, well-formed, and possess proud and expressive features of great beauty, which are strictly of the Aryan cast. They are honest, brave, generous and magnanimous. They wear the beard very long, divided into two pointed whiskers, which forms the distinctive peculiarity of almost every Rajpoot. Their only profession is that of arms. They are very courageous, good horsemen and intrepid hunters. The poorest Rajpoot of this day retains all the pride of

ancestry. He scorns to hold the plough or to use his lance
but on horse-back. The martial Rajpoots are not strangers
to armorial bearings, now so indiscriminately used in
Europe. Their costume is very elegant and their turbans
are very gracefully folded. Their girdles are always orna-
mented with a regular armoury of daggers, dirks and
swords. Their women are tall, well-made, and very pretty;
and are generally shut up in the zenana. Their costume is
very graceful. The Rajpoots now invest themselves with
the title of *Kshatriya*, a name which was formerly applied
to the warlike Aryan race.

Having thus given a bare outline of the History of
Rajpootana and a rough sketch of the Rajpoots, I shall
now take up the nineteen states contained in it, one by one,
and narrate the history of each as simply and briefly as
convenient.

The sum-total of the annals of these states will furnish
the reader a more detailed history of the whole of the
province of Rajpootana.

CHAPTER I.

Marwar or Jodhpur.

The early history of Marwar is wrapt in obscurity; still
there is reason to believe that the Jats, the *Minas* and the
Bhils held the country in separate chiefships before the
great *Rahtore* conquest. In 1194, Jey Chand, king of
Kanauj, was defeated by Mahamud Ghori. He died soon
after of a broken heart. Sheojee, grandson of Jey Chand,
entered Marwar on a pilgrimage to Dwarka, and, at the

entreaty of the local Brahman community, settled among them and became their protector. The Rahtore chief, acquiring land and power around Pali, the land of his first settlement, gained there the first footing in his future kingdom. His son and successor conquered the land of Kher from the *Gohel* Rajpoots, and established his brother, Soning, in Edar near Gujrat. It was Rao Chanda, the tenth in succession from Sheojee, who succeeded in gaining Mandur, then the capital of Marwar. From the time of Rao Chanda, A. D. 1382, that the actual conquest of Marwar by the Rahtores may be dated. Chanda was succeeded by Rao Rir Mall, a famous warrior as well as king. Jodha, the youngest of his twenty-four sons, ruled after him, and founded the city of Jodhpur, which he made his capital. He had fourteen sons, and from their progeny the principal *Rahtore* clans and feudal chiefs of Marwar were founded and the whole land overspread. Jodha Rao died in 1489 and was succeeded by his eldest son, Satel, who met his death in 1492. His successor was Rao Suja, the second son of Jodha Rao, who ruled over Marwar for 27 years. Rao Ganga succeeded on the death of his grandfather. He fought under Rana Sanga against Babar in 1527 in the fatal battle of Fateypur Sikri. Rao Ganga was succeeded by Rao Maldeo in 1532, during whose reign Marwar attained to its zenith of power, territory and independence. Emperor Humayon, when driven from the throne by Sher Shah, sought the protection of Maldeo ; but the Rao refused to shelter him. He did not get any benefit from this inhospitality. For Sher Shah came against him and defeated him. In 1561, Akbar in revenge for Maldeo's inhospitable treatment of his father, invaded Marwar and captured Mairta and Nagore and confered them on the younger branch of the family, the chief of Bikaneer, now established in independence of the parent State.

Chander Sen succeeded his father, Maldeo, in exclusion of the elder brother Oodey Sing, who was disliked by him and his nobles for his submission to Akbar. But Chander Sen was slain by Oodey Sing, who then obtained possession of the *gaudi,* and gave his sister, Jodh Bai, in marriage to Akbar. Oodey Sing was richly rewarded by the Emperor, and received the rank of Raja from him in 1584. He died in 1596 and was succeeded by his son, Sur Sing, who like his father attained to high honor with Akbar and for whom he conquered Gujrat and the Deccan. Jeswant Sing, the second son and successor of Raja Sur opposed Aurungzebe in his attempt to get the imperial throne, for which the latter, when emperor, never forgave him. To get rid of him, he was sent against the Afgans. He died beyond Attock, leaving as his successor, an infant son, Ajit, in 1681.

Aurungzebe attempted to seize the person of the young Ajit, but could not succeed. The prince was carried in safety to a place of concealment among the Marwar hills.

Aurungzebe invaded Marwar and plundered Jodhpur and sacked all the large towns. The Rajpoots of different clans united and defeated him in 1680-81. He then res tored Ajit to the *gaudi* of Marwar. In 1710, Shah Alum made friendship with the chief and restored the nine districts wrested from him by Aurungzebe. A daughter of Ajit Sing was given in marriage to emperor Ferrok Syar. To this marriage may be ascribed the rise of the British Power in India. The Emperor had a bad disease on the back, which was cured by the English surgeon, Mr.

Hamilton, who on asking to name his reward, obtained the firman conferring territorial possession and commercial privileges on the English. Ajit Sing was murdered by his son, Bakht Sing. But Abhoy Sing, the elder, succeeded to the throne in 1725. A quarrel arose between the two brothers and Abhoy Sing was killed. Ram Sing, son of Abboy Sing, became the Raja, but he was forced to take refuge in Ujjein being defeated by his uncle, Bakht Sing, at Mairta. Bukht Sing, the parricide, met his death of a poisoned robe, and Bejoy Sing, his son, gained the *gaudi*.

Hardly pressed by the Mahrattas, he ceded to them the district of Ajmere. For several years from this time Marwar enjoyed peace. But the Mahrattas under De Boigne and Sindia began again to molest the kingdom of Marwar. The Rajpoots united and defeated the Mahrattas under De Boigne at the battle of Tonga, and compelled Sindia to give up his conquests. Bejoy Sing recovered Ajmere temporarily, but was totally defeated by De Boigne at Patan and Mairta in succession in 1791, the result of which was the imposition of a contribution of £600,000. In 1794 Bejoy Sing died and was succeeded by Bhim Sing, who died in 1804, and was succeeded by Raja Man Sing, who ruled over Marwar for forty years. A quarrel arose between him and the Raja of Jeypore for the hand of Kristna Kumari, the fair maid of Oodeypore and Man Sing was defeated and beseiged in Jodhpur. The Rana poisoned the maid to restore peace to Rajpootana. For the murder of the chief of the *Naths*, Man Sing became a recluse and nominated his son, Chatur Sing, as his successor. A treaty was concluded in 1818 by which Jodhpur was taken under the protection of the British Government. Chator Sing died shortly after the conclusion of the treaty and his father received the administration.

Internal dissensions continued in Jodhpur, and the British Government was compelled to interfere. Man Sing died in 1843 and was succeeded by Takht Sing of Ahmednagore. Owing to constant disputes between the Jodhpur Durbar and the Thakurs, the affairs of Marwar remained in an unsatisfactory state during the administration of Maharaja Takht Sing, who was avaricious, careless of affairs and difficult of access. But he was a loyal chief and did good service during the mutiny. The right of adoption was duly bestowed upon the Maharaja Takht Sing who died in 1873 and was succeeded by his eldest son Maharaja Jeswant Sing, the present ruler of Marwar.

His Highness the Maharaja of Jodhpur, manages the affairs of his Raj with the help of his brothers, one of whom, Maharaja Sir Partap Sing, is the Prime Minister, and another, Maharaja Kishori Sing, is the commander-in-chief of the Jodhpur forces. Maharaja Jeswant Sing is kind-hearted, able and good, and has been created a G.C.S.I.

Since this time there has been no change of importance in the administration of Marwar. Maharaja Colonel Sir Partap Sing, the prime Minister, visited England in 1887, and during his absence the Maharaja looked more closely into the government of the state.

Jodhpur was visited in February 1888, by the Maharaja of Mysore who made a tour through part of Rajpootana, and he was most hospitably received and entertained.

His Highness the Maharaja of Jodhpur is entitled to a salute of nineteen guns.

The revenue of Jodhpur is about Rupees 17,50,000.

CHAPTER. II.

Bikaneer.

The founder of the Bikaneer State was Biku, the sixth son of Jodha Rao, who founded Jodhpur, and belonged to the Rahtore tribe of Rajpoots. He was born in 1439. In 1458, he led an expedition into the country now known as Bikaneer, then occupied by the *Jats* and other tribes. The quarrels among the Jat clans facilitated the conquest of the country. Biku founded the city of Bikaneer in 1488, and conquered additional territories from the *Bhattes*, a rival Rajpoot clan. He died in 1505 and was succeeded by Nankaran. The new prince wrested many districts from the *Bhattes*. He was succeeded by Jetsi, who enlarged his borders. Kalyan Sing, his eldest son, followed him, and then came his eldest born, Rai Sing, in 1573. During his reign Bikaneer rose to importance, and Rai Sing became a satrap of the Emperor Akbar his brother-in-law. Akbar conferred on him the title of Raja, and gave him the government of Hissar. Raja Rai Sing completely conquered the *Jats*, who sank to the position of labourers or serfs. Rai Sing distinguished himself in the seige of Ahmedabad, and married his daughter to Prince Selim, afterwards Emperor Jehangir. Rai Sing died in 1632, and was succeeded by his only son, Karan, who supported the claims of Dara against Aurungzebe. He died in 1674, and was followed by Anup Sing. He was appointed to govern Bejapore and Aurungabad by the Mogul Emperor, went with Raja Jeswant Sing of Jeypore to Cabul, returned and died at Bikaneer in 1709. Sarup Sing, his son, succeeded him. He was killed in attempting to take the castle and land of Adoni. He was succeeded by Sujan Sing, who again was succeeded by Zorawar Sing, both of whom were men of no note.

Raja Guj Sing got the *gaudi* next and reigned for forty-one years. He was engaged in border contests with the *Bhattes* and with Bhawalpur. He had sixty-one children. He was succeeded in 1787 by his son, Raj Sing, who was murdered by the mother of Sarat Sing, who at once assumed the office of Regent, and after having killed all who had prior right to the Bikaneer *musnud*, became its ruler in 1801. He was involved in the Jodhpur civil war, and, being unsuccessful in it, became oppressive to his people. Before his death in 1828, Bikaneer was embraced in the general scheme of subsidiary alliances, formed by the British Government at the time of the Pindari War. Ruttun Sing succeeded him, and proceeded to invade Jeysulmere for former injuries. Jodhpur and Jeypore assembled their forces in their respective frontiers and the peace of Rajpootana was threatened.

British Government interfered, and, through the arbitration of the Rana of Oodeypore, the dispute was settled. Raja Ruttun Sing died in 1852, and was succeeded by Sirdar Sing, who did good service in the mutiny, for which he received a grant of forty-one villages and the right of adoption. Sirdar Sing died in 1872 and was succeeded by Maharaja Dungar Sing, who was adopted by the Dowager Maharani. His late Highness was an able prince. On the 19th August, 1887, Maharaja Dungar Singh, who had been ailing for sometime, died childless at the age of thirty-three years. Shortly before his death, His Highness had adopted his younger brother, Gunga Sing, a boy about seven years old. The succession was recognized by the

Government of India and Gunga Sing was placed on the *gaudi* on the 31st August, 1887.

During the minority, the administration of the State has been placed in the hands of the Political Agent aided by a Council of Regency, and the various branches of the executive have been allotted to *Seghas* or departments.

The finances are in good order, there being an accumulated saving of 20 lakhs of rupees in hand.

His Highness is entitled to a salute of 17 guns.

The revenue of Bikaneer is about Rupees 6,00,000 .

CHAPTER III.

Jeypore.

The legendary founder of the royal family of Jeypore was descended from *Kush*, second son of Ram, who ruled at Ayodhya, and who is said to have migrated thence to Rhotas on the river Sone, whence after several generations a second migration brought Raja Nal westward across the Jumna to Narwar in 295. At Narwar the family established itself, until Dhola Rao founded Amber in A. D. 957, the former capital of the principality of Jeypore. The Jeypore family is known as the *Cutchwa* or *Kushwa* clan of Rajpoots. Dhola Rao conquered the country owned then by several petty Rajpoot and Mina chiefs, and founded the kingdom inherited by his descendants. He married the daughter of the king of Ajmere. He was succeeded by his son, Kankal, who, in his turn, was succeeded by his son, Maidal Rao, a warrior and conqueror, and he, in his turn, by Hundeo. Kuntal followed him, who subjugated the remaining tribes of the *Minas*. His successor, Pajun, was a famous Maharaja.

He celebrated himself in many exploits, defeated Mahamed
Ghori in the Khybar Pass and enabled, Prithvi Raj, king
of Delhi, to carry off the princess of Kanauj. His immediate successors were men of no distinction. Their names
were Mabsi, Bijul, Rajdeo, Kitnu, Kuntal, Junsi, Oodey
Karan, Nursing, Bunbir, Udharun and Khundrasen. The
ascent to the throne of Jeypore by Raja Prithi Raj marks
an era in the dynasty. Prithi Raj had seventeen sons, of
whom twelve lived long, and to these twelve and their
descendants he limited the future right of succession to
the throne. The twelve families of his twelve sons, he
styled the twelve *Kotris* or chambers of the Cutchwa House
of Rajpoots, one of the thirty-six royal races of Rajpoots.
From Prithi Raj we come down to Bahar Mull in 1548,
the first prince who paid homage to the Mahomedan power.
His son Bhagwan Dass, who ascended the throne in 1574,
served Akbar and gave his daughter in marriage to Selim
afterwards Emperor Jehangir. Bhagwan Doss was succeeded by his nephew, Man Sing, in 1590, who proved a
glory to the dynasty. He conquered Orissa for Akbar
and made Assam and Cabul tributaries to the Mugal
Empire. He ruled in succession Bengal, Behar, the
Deccan and Cabul. He assisted Khusra, his consin, for
getting possession of the throne against his father, Jehangir. He died in 1615 and was succeeded by his eldest son,
Jagat Sing I, who reigned till 1622. He was a celebrated
military commander. Second after Jagat Sing came Jey
Sing I, nephew to Raja Man Sing, in 1622. He was a
prince of great promise and is known as Mirza Raja. He
restored the glories of the family name. He performed
great services under the Emperor Aurungzebe. He imprisoned Sevaji, but afterwards finding that this pledge of

safety was likely to be broken, he assisted him to escape. Thus he incurred the wrath of the Emperor who sought to kill him. Jey Sing was poisoned by his younger son, Kireet Sing, under the orders of the Emperor Aurungzebe. Jey Sing was succeeded by his eldest son, Ram Sing, who and his heir, Bishan Sing, were princes of little mark. Bishan Sing was succeeded by Jey Sing II, better known as Sewae Jey Sing, in 1699. He served with distinction in the Deccan. On the death of Aurungzebe, he sided with Prince Bidar Bukht, son of Prince Azim, and a battle was fought at Dholpur in 170 7, in which Bahadur became victorious and Emperor of Delhi. For his enmity to the Emperor, Jeypore was sequestered ; but Jey Sing II came sword in hand and retook it. A triple alliance was formed among the Rajpoot Princes of Jeypore, Jodhpur and Meywar for mutual defence against the Mugals. Jey Sing II was a learned Maharaja. He was fond of Arts, Science and Mathematics. He was equal in astronomical knowledge to the European Astronomers of the day. He drew up a set of tables from which almanacs are still made. He caused Euclid's Geometry, the best treatise on plain and spherical Trigonometry, and Napier's Logarithms to be translated into Sanskrit. He built the new city of Jeypore on a regular plan for his capital, and erected observatories and invented many instruments for calculation. Unsuccessful in inspiring the Emperor Ferocksher with energy, he left the imperial court, and devoted himself to the study of astronomy and history. In 1720 when Mahamad Shah became emperor, Jey Sing was appointed governor of Agra and Malwa in succession. He procured the repeal of the *Jezia* and repressed the incursions of the Jats. In 1732, he was reappointed governor of Malwa, checked the aggressions of the Mahrattas and delayed their advance on the capital. He died in 1743 after a wise and prosperous reign of forty-four years. He was succeeded by Isri Sing. But the claim to the throne was contested by his younger brother, Madhu Sing, son of a Princess of Meywar, who according to a contract made with Oodeypore, had the right on his side.

Madhu Sing succeeded in getting the throne in 1751, and would have proved a good ruler but for the incursions of the *Jats*. He died very soon. He had many qualities of his illustrious father. He built many cities of which Madhupore near the celebrated fortress of Runthumbor is the most noted.

Prithi Sing II succeeded him in 1778, who again was succeeded by Partab Sing in 1779. He ruled the country for twenty-five years. During his minority Jeypore suffered greatly from the Mahrattas. On attaining his majority, he leagued himself with the Maharaja of Jodhpur and defeated the Mahrattas at Tonga in 1787. But this triumph was short-lived. He sustained defeats at Patan and Mairta in 1791, and from that period to 1803, the country was desolated by the Mahrattas. He died in 1803, and was succeeded by Raja Jagat Sing II, who ruled Jeypore for sixteen years. He sought in vain the hand of Kristna Kumari, the beautiful daughter of the Rana of Oodeypore, though it provoked a contest which threatened ruin to Rajpootana. He died in 1818. Though there happened no great event in this reign, but a treaty was concluded with the paramount British Government in 1803, which did not last long. But in 1818 through the mediation of Sir David Ochterlony, the subsidiary alliance was again formed and British protection was extended to Jeypore. Jagat Sing II died without issue in 1818, but one of the widowed queens was discovered to be pregnant. The son born of this *Rani* was named Jey Sing III,who did not live long. During his short and uneventful reign, Jeypore was a scene of corruption and misrule. He died in 1835, leaving an infant son, aged two years, afterwards the illustrious Maharaja Sewae Ram Sing II. The Agent, Governor-General, Rajpootana, came to Jeypore to reform the administration and assumed the guardianship of the infant Prince left by the Raja. The strong measures he adopted led to the formation of a conspiracy by the Singhi Jhutharam. The life of the Agent, Colonel Alves, was attempted, and his assistant, Mr. Blake, was murdered. The murderers were seized and executed. The young Maharaja, Sewae Ram Sing II, was placed under the guardianship of the Political Agent. Under his superintendence a council of regency was formed. The army was reduced. Every branch of administration was reformed, and *Sati*, slavery and infanticide were prohibited, and the annual tribute was reduced to four lacs in 1842. Maharaja Ram Sing got the administration of his Raj into his own hands in 1854 when he arrived at the age of majority. His Highness did good service during the mutiny, for which he got the district of Kot-Kassim from the British Government. He also received the right of adoption. Maharaja Ram Sing was an intelligent Prince and devoted his best energies to the development of the resources of his country. His Highness opened out new roads, constructed railways, introduced water-pipes, lighted the city with gas, and gave a great impulse to education. In 1868, during a great scarcity, he abolished transit duties on the importation of grains into his dominions. He intelligently managed the affairs of his country. He increased the beauty of Jeypore by additional buildings, and constructed hospitals and other public institutions. He was honored with the title of G. C. S. I. He was extremely fond of the society of cultivated Englishmen and women. He twice became a member of the Legislative council of the Viceroy and Governor-General of India. His Highness Maharaja Sewae Ram Sing II., G. C. S. I., ruled wisely, vigourously and prosperously. He loved his subjects and servants as his children and was loved by them in return.

"Maharaja Ram Singjee ruled the land,
With justice and with no merciless hand;
With Council's help, he guided the state barge,
The people he loved, and his heart was large.
To them his heart, his love, his griefs were given,
But all his serious thoughts had rest in heaven."

A Poem on "Jeypore" by *A. L. De.*

This illustrious and beloved Maharaja died on the 18th day of September, 1880, after having reigned for a period of about forty-five years. His Highness was succeeded by his adopted son, Maharaja Sewae Madhu Sing II, the present ruler of Jeypore. His Highness is an intelligent Prince and is treading the footsteps of his illustrious and lamented predecessor.

During his minority, the Jeypore principality was ruled by the Jeypore Council under the joint-presidentship and supervision of the Resident. His Highness has now got the administration of his Raj into his own hands, and has been created a G. C. S. I., in August 31, 1888.

His Highness the Maharaja is ably managing the affairs of the state with the aid of the Council and especially by the advice of Baboo Kantee Chander Mookerjee, chief member, Jeypore Council, whose administrative ability and integrity have been generally acknowledged.

Reforms have lately been introduced in the Judicial Departments of the State, and measures have been adopted for the reclamation of the *Minas*, while illicit opium traffic with the Punjab has been carefully watched.

The state barge is safely and ably steered, and life and property are quite secure here, so that as was said of the reigns of Bikramaditya and Akbar, it may be said too of this reign, that an old woman may carry gold openly in her hands any where in Jeypore *unprotected*.

His Highness is entitled to a salute of 19 guns.

The revenue of Jeypore is about Rupees 4,000,000.

CHAPTER IV.

Jeysulmere.

The founder of Jeysulmere was Rawal Jeysal, a prince of the *Bhattes*, a branch of the Jadu race, the patronymic of the descendants of the *Budha*, the ancestor of the *Somabungsa* or Lunar race. The power of this race was paramount in India 3000 years ago. This branch of the Jadu race wandered through different parts of India and Afganisthan, and, at last, under their Rawal Deoraj, founded and settled in Deorawal. Deoraj conquered Lodorva, capital of the Lodra Rajpoots, and made it his own. Jeysal, sixth in discent from Deoraj, considering that city to be insecure, built a new one ten miles distant from it, which he named Jeysulmere after him, and made it his capital in 1156.

Jeysal was succeeded by Salibahan, a great and success-

D.

ful warrior. He was killed when fighting against the
Beluchis. Bejil succeeded him but ruled only for a short
time. He was followed by his uncle, Kalyan, who defeated
the Beluchis and slew their leader. He ruled for nineteen
years prosperously. He was succeeded by his son, Chachick
Deo, in 1219, who ruled over Jeysulmere for thirty-two
years. He was succeeded by his grandson, Karan, who
ruled for twenty-eight years, and was a valiant and successful monarch like his predecessor. Lakhur Sen succeeded him. He was a foolish ruler and held power for four
years only, and was replaced by his son, Pompal. This ruler
was of a violent temper, and was therefore replaced by
Jetsi, the elder brother of Rawal Karan. Jetsi reigned for
eighteen years and died on the eighth year of the seige
of Jeysulmere made by the Emperor Alla-ud-din, and
was succeeded by his son, Mulraj. The seige of the city
was continued in his reign, and such was the distress
suffered by the inhabitants, that Mulraj and his army,
having sacrificed all the females, rushed out of the city ;
and, having inflicted a great slaughter upon the foe, were
destroyed to a man in 1295.

The city remained for two years in the possession of
the Moslems. It was then seized by the *Rahtores* of
Meywar, who were very soon driven out by the remaining
Bhattes led on by Dadu, son of Jeysur, who was elected
Rawal. Dadu carried off the horses of the Emperor of
Delhi and was beseiged in his capital in 1306 by the
Emperor, who committed greater havoc to the city than
had been done in the preceeding seige. The names of the
successors of Dadu were Garsi, Kehur, Kailem, Chachick
Deo, Bersi, Jait, Nunkarun, Bhim, Manahar Dass and
Sabul Sing, who were rulers of minor importance. Amru

Sing succeeded Sabul. He cleared the country of robbers and defeated the designs of the Raja of Bikaneer upon his kingdom. He was succeeded in 1702 by Jeswant Sing. During his unfortunate reign, Pugul, Barmair, Fellodi and other towns were wrested from him by the Rahtores, and the territory near Garah by Dawud Khan. He was succeeded by his son, Akhi Sing, who again was followed by Mulraj in 1762. Sarup Sing, his minister, was a wicked man and offended the crown prince and was murdered by him. For a time misrule devastated the land. Salim Sing, Sarup Sing's son, was made minister, who was as bad as his father. He revenged his father's death by killing the heir-apparent and other princes and princesses, and filled the land with sin and woe. In 1818 however the state was placed under British protection. In 1820, Mulraj died and was succeeded by his grandson, Guj Sing. But till 1824 when Salim Sing died, his career of cruelty, extortion and misgovernment was continued. After this minister's death, Guj Sing by measures of just and conciliatory nature, gained great popularity with his people. He made friendship with Bikaneer and the British Government. In 1844, after the conquest of Sindh, the forts of Shagarh, Gursia and Gatura were restored to Jeysulmere.

Guj Sing died in 1846, and was succeeded by Ranjit Sing, who in 1862 received a *Sanad* guaranteeing him the right of adoption. He died in 1864. The present chief Maharawal Bairisal, brother of Ranjit Sing, succeeded him in 1864, having been adopted by the widow of Ranjit Sing who died without heirs.

As the young prince Bairisal was only fifteen years old, the affairs of the Jeysulmere Raj were administered by his father, Thakur Kaisri Sing. In October, 1865,

Maharawal Bairisal took the reins of Government into his own hands, his father whose administration had given satisfaction to all continuing as minister. The Maharawal of Jeysulmere is entitled to a salute of fifteen guns, and has been granted the right of adoption.

The revenue of Jeysulmere is about Rupees 500,000.

CHAPTER V.

Meywar or Oodeypore.

The legendary founder of the Meywar dynasty was Kenksen, the sixty-third in descent from Lob, son of Ram, the ancient Maharaja of Ayodhya or Oudh, who is said to have emigrated in A. D. 145, from the Punjab to Gujrat, where his descendants reigned at Bullabhi until it was destroyed in 524. One of the Princes of the dynasty escaped destruction, and ruled at Edar. The Bhils of that country tired of a foreign rule, killed the eighth prince, but his infant son, Bappa, afterwards Bappa Rawal, was preserved. He grew up amidst the wilderness of the Aravallis and took refuge with the *Mori* chief of Chitor. He it was that led the Chitor forces against the Mahomedans on their first invasion of India from Sindh; and, after defeating and expelling them, he was joined by the nobles. He seized Chitor and founded the kingdom his descendants hold to the present day. Little is known of its history till 1150 when we come to Somarsi, the brother-in-law of Prithvi Raj, who was killed by Mohamad Ghori in 1193.

Karna succeeded Somarsi, and his son, Mahap, was driven from Chitor by his brother-in-law, the chief of

Jhalor. Mahap resigned his claim to the throne of Chitor and is said to have founded the State of Dungarpur. Chitor was recovered by his uncle, Bharat, in 1201 who placed his son, Rahab, on its throne. He changed the title of the tribe to *Sesodia*, and that of its ruler from Rawal to Rana. In the short space of fifty years, six Ranas were killed in battle fighting for the recovery of Gya.

Lakhamsi succeeded and began his rule over Meywar in 1275, and it was during his reign in 1290 that Chitor was stormed and sacked by Alla-ud-din Khilji for its fair Queen, Padmani. The Rana died in defending the city, but his son, Ajeysi, escaped to Kailwara, and at his death in 1301, his nephew, Hamir, became his successor. Hamir married the daughter of the Jhalor chief, Maldeo, who held Chitor for the Mahomedans, and by her means retook it. He extended his authority over the surrounding chiefs and clans, and left a name behind him still honored in Meywar as a very wise and gallant prince.

Kaitsi who succeeded Hamir, conquered the hill-districts of Meywar. He was succeeded by Lakha in 1373 during whose reign the rich lead and silver mines of Jawar were discovered, and their proceeds expended in rebuilding the temples and palaces levelled by Alla-ud-din. Lakha was succeeded by Mokul who was assassinated and followed by Khumbhu in 1419. The reign of Khumbhu was one of great success amid no ordinary difficulties. He defeated the Mahomedan kings of Malwa at Gujrat, erected the triumphal pillar at Chitor in commemoration of his splendid victories. He reigned prosperously for fifty years. He fell by the hand of his son, Oodey. He bestowed Ajmere and Sambhar on Jodhpur, made the

Deòra Prince independent on Abu, and offered a daughter in marriage to the Emperor of Delhi; but he was killed by lightning before he had time to complete the disgrace. His sons disputed the throne with Raemal, who succeeded him in 1474. One of his sons was killed and the other founded the State of Partapgarh.

Raemul was succeeded by his son, the famous Rana Sanga, in 1509, under whom Meywar reached the summit of glory and prosperity. Rana Sanga opposed the Emperor Babar and was defeated by him at the battle of Fateypur Sikri in 1527. He survived his defeat only for a short time. Rana Ratna, his son, succeeded him. He was killed in a feud by the Bundi Rao and was succeeded in 1535 by Bikramjit. Bikramjit was a proud prince and alienated the attachment of his subjects. Bahadur, king of Gujrat, invaded Meywar, attacked Chitor and took it after a long seige. Emperor Humayon came to the relief of Bikramjit and restored him to his capital. Banbir deposed him and usurped the throne for a short time. He was deposed by Oodey Sing, the younger son of Rana Sanga. During his reign, Chitor was attacked, taken and demolished by the Emperor Akbar in 1568. Chitor now remains a ruined monument of the glories of the past. Oodey Sing, on the loss of his capital, founded Oodeypore, thenceforth the capital of Meywar. He was succeeded by his son Partap Sing, whose name is still idolized by every Rajpoot as the upholder of the fame of the Race. He was defeated by Prince Selim at the battle of Haldighat. Hemmed in by the armies of the Emperor, and all his forts conquered, he fled to the Punjab, but while on his flight, he got a large sum of money from his prime minister, Bhim Sing. He returned to his capital suddenly, reconquered the whole country, and retained it till his death.

Partap's son, Umra, succeeded him in 1579, and repeatedly defeated the imperial armies. The Emperor Jabangir came in person to the seat of war and forced Umra to submit. He abdicated the throne in 1621 in favour of Karasi who was succeeded by Jagat Sing in 1628, during whose reign tranquillity prevailed throughout the country. Jagat Sing adorned the new capital, repaired the walls and built the beautiful water-places in the lake. In the reign of his successor, Raj Sing, Aurungzebe intended to impose the jezia on all Hindus, and marched against the Rajpoots in person, but was repeatedly defeated. Peace was at last made with Jey Sing, successor of Raj Sing. Umra, who succeeded Jey Sing in 1700, formed an alliance, offensive and defensive, with Jeypore and Marwar, against the incursions of the Emperor of Delhi. But it did not last long. Umra died in 1716 and was succeeded by Sangram Sing, who was again succeeded by Jagat Sing II, in 1734. At this period the Mahrattas began to invade Rajpootana. In 1736, Baji Rao, their Peshwa, forced the Rana to pay him annually Rupees 160,000. For getting assistance from Holkar in a family quarrel with Jeypore, the Rana made over Rampura to Holkar.

Partap Sing II was succeeded by Jagat II, who was followed in 1762 by Ursi. During the reign of this Rana, Meywar was repeatedly invaded by the Mahrattas, and he was forced to cede to them the districts of Jawud, Jiran and Nimuch, and to the Raja of Marwar the province of Godwar to preserve it from the pretender, Ratna. Ursi was murdered by the Raja of Bundi and was succeeded by his infant son, Hamir. Hamir died young in 1778 and was succeeded by his brother, Bhim Sing, the commencement of whose reign was marked by sanguinary feuds amongst the nobles, which rendered his country an easy prey to the Mahrattas. In 1806, the distractions were increased by a ruinous war between Jeypore and Marwar for the hand of the Rana's fair daughter, Kristna Kumari, whose tragic death is a fit subject for a romance. She was sacrificed by the Rana for the peace of Rajpootana. From this time till 1817, Meywar was ravaged by the Mahrattas and the Pindari Amir Khan, and peace and prosperity left the country. In 1817, the British Government resolved to extend British protection over the States of Rajpootana and it entered into a treaty with the Rana. For this treaty and other treaties between the British Government and the Native States of Rajpootana, vide Aitchison's *Treaties*. Captain Tod was the first agent appointed to Oodeypore on behalf of the British Government, and he was directed to take charge of affairs of the Oodeypore Raj into his own hands.

Bhim Sing died in 1828 and was succeeded by Jowan Sing who was a debauchee. He died in 1838 and was succeeded by his adopted son, Sirdar Sing, who was succeeded by his brother, Sarup Sing. The country grew poor every day and the imperial tribute was reduced. Sarup Sing died in 1861, and was succeeded by his adopted son, Sumbhoo Sing. During his minority the State was governed by the Political Agent, who improved the prospects of the country. Maharana Sumbhoo Sing got the management of the affairs of the State on attaining his majority in 1865. He died in 1874 and was succeeded by his first cousin Sujjan Sing. During his minority the affairs of the State were managed by a council of Regency aided by the advice of the Political Agent. Maharana

Sujjan Sing, G. C. S. I., was entrusted with the administration of the State in 1876. He attempted to rule well
and secure to His Highness's subjects peace and prosperity,
but unfortunately died very soon. He was succeeded by
His Highness the Maharana, Futtey Sing, Bahadur, G.
C. S. I., who is now ruling the State of Oodeypore peacefully, vigorously and prosperously. Maharana Futtey
Sing has got two sons, the second having been born in
November, 1887, which was made an occasion of much
rejoicing.

The new revenue settlement has been introduced in
the pergunnahs of Akola, Hurra, Shumbugarh, Chitore
and Rajnagar. His Highness has' received the right of
adoption and is entitled to a salute of 17 guns.

The revenue of Oodeypore is about Rupees 45,00,000.

CHAPTER VI.

Kotah.

Emperor Jahangir bestowed Kotah and its dependencies
in 1625 on Madhu Sing, the second son of Rao Rutton
of the State of Bundi, to be held by him and his heirs
direct of the crown. Thus was Kotah and its dependencies
severed for ever from Bundi, of which it was a dependency.
Madhu Rao, its first ruler, assumed the rank and title of
Raja and ruled for many years. He extended his principality to Malwa on one side and Bundi on the other.
Makund Sing, his eldest son, succeeded him in 1657. At
the battle of Ujjein fought in 1658 for the empire of India,
Makund Sing and his four brothers took the side of the
rightful heir to the throne of Delhi, and all the brothers

fell except Kishore Sing the youngest.   Makund Sing was
succeeded by his son, Jagat Sing, who reigned for twelve
years, passed with the imperial army in the Deccan, and
was succeeded by his cousin, Prem Sing. The new Raja
proved a stupid and worthless ruler, and was replaced by
Kishore Sing, youngest brother of Raja Makund Sing.
He distinguished himself in the service of the Moguls in
the Deccan and was slain at the escalade of Arcot. He
was succeeded by his second son, Ram Sing, who sided
Prince Azim against Bahadur Shah, and was slain at the
battle of Jajoo in 1707. Bhim Sing succeeded him and
supported the cause of the Sayeds against their masters
and was highly rewarded by them. He assisted Jey Sing
of Jeypore to expel the royal family of Bundi and annexed
many districts by expelling the Bhils from their fortresses.
Raja Bhim got the title of " Leader of five thousand"
and that of "Maharao." He was slain while attempting
to capture Nizam-ul-mulk, Subadar of the Deccan. Arjun
Sing his eldest son succeeded him and reigned for four
years. He died without issue and was succeeded by his
third brother, Durjan Sal, his second brother having been
killed in the civil war between the brothers. Durjan Sal
was a successful ruler. He conciliated Baji Rao the
Peshwa and got Nahrgarh as a reward for services done.
He aided the heir of the royal family of Bundi to recover
his ancestral possessions and successfully defended Kotah
against all inroads of the Raja of Jeypore. Durjan Sal
died without issue and was succeeded by Ajit Sing, a
descendant of Bishan Sing, the disinherited eldest son of
Raja Ram Sing. He reigned only for two years and a
half, and was succeeded by his son, Chattar Sal. During
the reign of this Maharao and the subsequent four reigns,

Zalim Sing remained Prime Minister of the Kotah Raj. Zalim Sing was a wonderful man, fond of power, unscrupulous to the means he used, possessed of keen and vivid intellect, courageous, full of resources and powerful to subdue all difficulties. Throughout the four reigns he lived to see, he ruled Kotah all-powerfully like Thomas-a-Becket of England. In the reign of Maharao Chattar Sal, the Raja of Jeypore again attacked Kotah, but through the unsurpassed skill and stratagem of Zalim Sing, he was forced to retire, his troops having fled from fear of being plundered by Mulhar Rao Holkar, who was excited to attack the Jeypore camp by the cunning Zalim Sing.

Chattar Sal was succeeded by his brother, Guman Sing, who was a distinguished prince, full of vigor and intellect; but he was unfortunately involved in a quarrel with his minister Zalim Sing who had crossed him in love.

Zalim Sing was forced to leave Kotah and take refuge in Oodeypore where he was welcomed, the Maharana having been through his instrumentality relieved from the bondage of one of his vassals, the chieftain of Delwara. Some-time after Zalim Sing returned and was well-received by his master, as he had become afraid of the Mahrattas. Guman Sing was succeeded by his son, Umed Sing, with the title of Maharao, but Zalim Sing became the real master of the State. He ruled over Kotah for forty-five years, and during his administration, it was respected by the Mahomedans, the Mahrattas, and the Rajpoots, and it secured some additional districts. He was a successful ruler and was celebrated for justice and good faith.

In 1817 Zalim Sing placed the State of Kotah under the protection of the British Power by a treaty containing the usual terms with an additional article vesting the administration of Kotah in Zalim Sing and his heirs. Umed Sing died in 1820 and was succeeded by his son, Kishore Sing. No sooner he sat on the throne, he did not like to be a nominal ruler and quarrelled with Zalim Sing. A battle was fought at Mangral in 1821, in which the Maharao was defeated. He took shelter in Jodhpur, but returned soon to his capital and recognized the perpetual rule of his minister and his heirs. Zalim Sing, who had already got the title of Raj Rana, died in 1824, and was succeeded by his son, Madhu Sing. In 1828, Kishore Sing died and was succeeded by his son, Ram Sing. Madhu Sing, the minister, died a little after, and was succeeded by his son, Madan Sing, with whom the Maharao was never in cordial relations. The quarrel got to such a pitch that at last Ram Sing was forced to create a new and independent principality for Madan Sing and his heirs, by separating seventeen districts from the State of Kotah, named Jhalawar, and was made over to Madan Sing.

Maharao Ram Sing died in 1866, and was succeeded by his son, Chutter Sing, the present chief. The State of Kotah is in a prosperous condition. The pains-taking care of Colonel Bayley is evident in every detail of the administration as well as in numerous improvements in the shape of public buildings, beautifully laid-out gardens, and other works of utility.

The Maharao manages his State by the advice of the Political Agent and with the assistance of a well-chosen council, who practically administer the affairs of government. He has received the right of adoption and is entitled to a salute of seventeen guns. The revenue of Kotah is about Rupees 2,500,000.

CHAPTER VII.

Ulwur.

Mewat, in the centre of which the city Ulwur is situated, and from which the whole province is named, is repeatedly mentioned by the Hindu bard, *Chand*, in -the
Prithvi Raj Rasa. Mohesh, Lord of Mewat, did homage
to Bissaldeo Chohan of Ajmere in 764; and his descendant
Mungal was defeated by Prithvi Raj. The lords of Mewat
were of the *Jadu* Rajpoot clan. Mention is made of Mewat
in the Turkish *Feroz Shahi.* Sayed Mubarik in 1424
ravaged rebellious Mewat. The first military movement
of Bahlol Lodi was made against Mewat then ruled over
by Ahmed Khan. In 1526, the Mewati chief, Hassan
Khan, assisted Rana Sanga in the great battle fought
against Babar. Babar states in his "Memoirs" that Hassan
Khan's ancestors had made their capital, Tijara, but when
he came to Mewat, Ulwur was found to be the seat of
government. Akbar visited Ulwur in 1579 on his way
to Fateypur Sikri. Sewae Jey Sing of Jeypore is said to
have obtained Ulwur in jagir from Aurungzebe. Udey
Karan, head of the Cachawa Rajpoot clan, ruled Jeypore
in 1367. His eldest son, Bar Sing, is the ancestor of the
present ruling house of Ulwur. Lala, third in descent
from Bar Sing, was the ancestor of the *Dasawat Narukas*,
to which the Ulwur family belongs. Rao Kalyan Sing,
fourth in descent from Lala, was the first of the *Lalawat
Narukas* to settle in the present Ulwur territory. Kalyan
Sing was sent by Sewae Jey Sing of Jeypore to rule
Kawa now in Bharatpur, but he returned to Macheri in
Mewat in 1671 unable to discharge his duties. Rao Anand
Sing, eldest son of Kalyan Sing, held Macheri. There

were two grandsons of Anand Sing, Zorawar Sing and
Zalim Sing. Zorawar Sing as head of the house remained
at Macheri and Zalim Sing received Bijwar. Rao Zorawar
Sing's grandson, Rao Partap Sing, developed his little
state into a principality by additional conquests and threw
off allegiance to Jeypore in 1774. Partap Sing about this
time assisted Mirza Najaf Khan in his war carried on
against the Jats and succeeded in defeating them at
Barsana and at Dig, and as a reward for this service
he obtained the title of Rao Raja and a *Sannad* for
Macheri to hold it direct from the crown. About this
time also he wrested from Bharatpur the strong hill fort
and fortified town of Ulwur and other places near its vici-
nity. To secure these newly-got possessions he fortified
all the commanding positions and held them by strong
garrisons. He died in 1794 and was succeeded by his
adopted son, Bhaktawar Sing. In his reign the Mahrattas
began to overrun and disturb Ulwur and the Rao Raja
thought it proper and safe to be placed under the protection of the British Government. Accordingly in 1806, a
treaty, offensive and defensive, was concluded with the
Paramount British Government. During the reign of
this Rao, he performed acts that were displeasing to the
British Power. He persecuted his Mahomedan subjects.
He made an embankment across the *Mahnas Nai* and
thereby prevented the free flow of water into the fields of
the neighbouring British subjects. He also attacked some
cities of other Native Princes contrary to the treaty with
the English. But he was forced at last to submit and
live peacefully. Rao Raja Bhaktawar Sing died in 1815
and was succeeded by his adopted son, Benoy Sing, who
was to enjoy the title, and his illegitimate son, Balwant

Sing, who should exercise the power of the State. The British Government sanctioned this arrangement. This state of things went on till the boy princes had grown up, when Benoy Sing imprisoned Balwant Sing and attempted to take the life of the head of the opposite faction. British Government interfered and he was brought to his senses. Like his predecessor he showed in some other acts of defiance but a threat of the march of British troops brought him to reason. He died in 1867 and was succeeded by his son, Seodan Sing. During his minority disputes took place between the Rajpoot nobles and his Mussalman ministers, and the ministers were driven away. The British Government formed a council of Regency to manage the State affairs assisted by the Political Agent. Sheodan Sing attained his majority in 1863, but he did not get the dress of investiture for frequent commotions in his State and for his misconduct till 1867, when the Governor-General's Agent having reported favourably of his administration, the dress of investiture was bestowed upon him.

Maharao Sheodan Sing died in 1874 and was succeeded by His Highness Maharao Mungal Sing, the present chief of Ulwur, who is carrying on the affairs of his Government ably and prosperously. The State of Ulwur is now in a very good order. The Chief takes a great interest in all that goes on in his State and particular pride in his troops and stables.

He has been fortunate in having had so capable and sound an officer as Colonel Peacock for many years as his Political Agent. He has received the right of adoption and is entitled to a salute of fifteen guns. The chief of Ulwur has lately been created a G. C. S. I., and a Maharaja.

The revenue of the State of Ulwur is about Rupees 1,600,000.

CHAPTER VIII.

Sirohee and *Abu*.

Sirohee.

Deoraj, son of Manji, a descendant of Prithvi Raj, the Chohan King of Delhi, was the ancestor of the present ruling family of Sirohee. They were *Deora* Rajpoots. The first inhabitants of Sirohee were the *Bhils*. After the Bhils, the *Gehlot* Rajpoots settled in Sirohee and were succeeded by the *Pramar* Rajpoots. The Pramars were succeeded by the *Chohans*, in 1152, who under Sohi Rao the Chohan leader established themselves along the western border of Sirohee. Deoraj was seventh in succession from Sohi Rao and the founder of the Sirohee royal family. Deoraj was succeeded by Pataji, who again was succeeded by Bigarji Rao. Sobhaji, third in descent from Bigarji, populated a city called Sirohee near the site of the present capital in 1405. His son, Sains Mal, who succeeded him, built in 1425 another city called also Sirohee, the present capital of the State. Sirohee is the only country in Rajpootana which remained independent acknowledging neither the suzerainty of the Mogal, Rahtore or Mahratta power. This country was inhabited by the *Bhils*, *Minas* and *Grasias*, who lived a life of lawlessness and licence among their native hills. The Rajas of Jodhpur attacked them repeatedly, but they never acknowledged themselves conquered. They were wild, savage and free in the beginning, and they remained so ever after. But dissensions among them weakened them in the beginning of the nineteenth century, when their Rao from being master and sovereign, became their oppressor. The name of the Rao was Oodeybanji. Many of the Thakores unable to bear his tyranny, transferred their allegiance to more genial lords. Some that remained revolted, deposed and imprisoned him. They appointed as Regent his brother Sheo Sing. Oodeybanji applied for aid to Maharaja Man Sing of Jodhpur, who availing himself of this long-wished-for opportunity, sent an expedition against Sirohee. But it retired baffled, beaten and humiliated. Oodeybanji soon died in confinement in 1846. The advantages of subsidiary league with Britain and its protection have been felt every-where throughout India and especially in the lawless and turbulent Rajpootana. Sheo Sing the Regent hastened te ask protection from the British Power no sooner he drove back the Jodhpur invading army. His prayers were granted. A treaty was concluded in 1823 with the British Government and British protection was extended to Sirohee. Sheo Sing was acknowledged as Rao and his son as heir-apparent in 1847. The Rao made over to the British Government some lands on Mount Abu for the establishment of a sanitarium fettered by certain conditions, one of which was that no kine should be killed there. In 1854, at the request of the Rao, the State was taken under British management. In 1857, it was under British management that the mutiny broke out. The Rao behaved very friendly on this occasion to the paramount power. In 1861, Sheo Sing died, and Oomed Sing his son succeeded him. The early years of this Rao were disturbed by his three brothers having rebelled against him, but they were soon forced to yield and live quietly. Nothing of importance happened in this reign afterwards. Rao Oomed Sing died at Sirohee in 1875, and was succeeded by Kesri Sing, who is now Rao of Sirohee. The government of this State has improved of late years and the Rao himself has done much to bring about this satisfactory state of things. Improved trade and communications bring His Highness in a larger revenue than formerly from Abu, and the Durbar has liberally consented to aid the Abu municipality with an annual contribution of Rupees 3000, thereby relieving the British Government of its grant-in-aid. The Rao of Sirohee has received the right of adoption and is entitled to a salute of 15 guns.

The revenue of Sirohee is about Rupees 80,900.

Abu.

Lieutenant-Colonel James Tod, formerly political agent in the Western Rajpootana and well-known as the author of the "Annals of Rajpootana," was the first European who visited Abu, and may be considered as the discoverer of Abu in the early part of the 19th century. He writes in his "Travels in Western India" that the discovery was his own and that he gave it a local habitation and a name. From 1822 to 1840 Abu was used as a summer residence by the political superintendent of Sirohee and the officers of the Jodhpur Legion. In 1840 it was first used as a residence during the summer season of invalid European soldiers. In 1843 barracks and hospitals were built, and about this time the Agent, Governor-General, Rajpootana, commenced to reside on Abu during the hot season, accompanied by his assistants and Office-establishment and the Vakils of the States of Rajpootana. In this way the station has gradually grown up, and the civil portion now consists of the Residency of the Agent, Governor-General, Rajpootana, and some forty scattered bungalows for his Officers, Vakils and visitors. The military sanitarium contains accommodation for about two hundred men, including quarters for twenty-six families.

Like most hill stations Abu is nearly empty during the cold season, when the Agent, Governor-General, Rajpootana, and his Staff, leave for their cold weather tour in the plains, while the European soldiers for the most part with-draw to Deesa.

In the district of Abu there are fifteen villages, a church, a club, the telegraph and post offices, and a hospital.

CHAPTER IX.

Ajmere-Marwara.

Ajmere.

The early history of Ajmere is legendary in its character. According to tradition, the fort and city of Ajmere were founded by Raja Aja, a descendant of Anhal, the first *Chohan* Rajpoot, in 145 A. D. He attempted to build a fort on Nagpahar, but not being able to fulfil his design there, he erected the present fort on Taragarh. He built a town in the valley of Inderkot, and called it Ajmere after his own name. The third in succession to him was Dolah Rao who opposed Mohamad Kassim and was slain by him in 685. His successor, Manik Rao, founded Sambhar and the *Chohan* princes thereafter adopted the title of Samri Rao. From his reign till 1024, we know nothing of the history of the *Chohan* Rajpoots of Ajmere. In 1024, Sultan Mahmud beseiged Ajmere then ruled by Bilumdeo and plundered it ; but could do no harm to Taragarh its fort. Bilumdeo was succeeded by Bisuldeo, who was a renowned Prince. He captured Delhi from the *Tuar* Rajpoots and subdued the hill-tribes of Marwara. He was succeeded by his grandson, Ana, who constructed the embankment which forms the Anasagar lake, on which Shah Jahan built a range of marble pavilions. Someswar, the third in descent from Ana, married the daughter of Anangpal, the *Tuar* king of Delhi and his son was the celebrated Prithvi Raj, the last of the Chohans, who was adopted by Anangpal, and thus became king of Ajmere and Delhi.

Prithvi Raj opposed Mahamad Ghori in his invasion of India in 1191 and 1193 A. D., and in the latter year at Thaneswar he was totally defeated by the Mussulman invader and was put to death in cold blood. After having placed a relative of Prithvi Raj on the throne of Delhi and Ajmere, Mahamad Ghori returned to his capital. A pretender to the throne of Ajmere in the person of Hemraj, put the new Raja of Ajmere to great perplexities. Kutub-ud-din, the founder of the Slave dynasty at Delhi, went to assist him and defeated Hemraj, and appointed a governor of his own faith to control the Raja of Ajmere. A few years afterwards the Raja of Ajmere uniting with the *Rahtores* and *Mers*, attempted independence, but failed in being successful. Kutub-ud-din shut him up in the fort. The Raja finding no means of escape, burnt himself by ascending the funeral pile. Kutub-ud-din then annexed the principality of Ajmere to the kingdom of Delhi and made over the charge of the fort Taragarh to

Sayed Hoshen, an officer of his own. On the death of Kutub-ud-din in 1210, the *Rahtores* and *Chohans* made a night attack upon the fort. The garrison taken unawares, was massacred to a man. Their tombs as well as those of Sayed Hoshen and his horse, may still be seen in the enclosure which bears the name of *Gunj Shahidan* or the Treasury of Martyrs. On the extinction of the House of Tuglak, Rana Kumbhu of Meywar attempted to take possession of Ajmere, but on his assassination, the territory fell into the hands of the kings of Malwa in 1469, and was held by them till the death of Mahmud II in 1531, when Ajmere was taken possession of by Maldeo Rahtore, king of Marwar.

He improved the fortress of Taragarh and began the construction of a *lift* to raise water to the fort from the adjacent *Nur Chusma* spring. But the scheme was never completed. The *Rahtores* held Ajmere for twenty-four years. On the accession of Akbar, it was annexed to the Mogul Empire; and from 1556 to the reign of Mahamad Shah, a period of 194 years, Ajmere remained an integral portion of it. During the reigns of the powerful Mogul Emperors, Ajmere gave its name to a *Subah*, which included the whole of Rajpootana, and formed an appanage of the Imperial residence, not only as a pleasant retreat, but also for keeping control over the surrounding chiefs. It was in Ajmere that Akbar lived when he made a pilgrimage to the tomb of the Saint *Khwaja Muen-ud-din Chisti*. It was at Ajmere that Jahangir received the English Envoy, Sir Thomas Roe, of James I, king of England, who reached the city in December, 1615. It was at Ajmere that Aurungzebe crushed the army of his unfortunate brother, Dara. And it was at Ajmere that he formed his head-quarters when he warred against Meywar and Marwar.

On the death of the Sayeds in 1720, Ajit Sing, king of Marwar, seized on Ajmere consequent on the decline of the Mogul Empire, coined money on his own name and set up every emblem of sovereign rule. Mohamad Shah collected a large army and invested Taragarh, and after four months, took possession of it and Ajmere. Ten years after, he appointed Abhoy Sing who assisted in the assassination of his father, Ajit Sing, as Viceroy of Ajmere. Abhoy Sing was succeeded by Ram Sing. Bakht Sing, the uncle of Ram Sing, defeated him in the battle of Mairta and took possession of Ajmere. Ram Sing sought the assistance of Jey Appa, the leader of the Mahrattas. Bakht Sing died of poison and was succeeded by his son Bejoy Sing, who was defeated by Jey Appa and fled to Nagor which withstood a year's seige. The Mahratta leader was murdered. But Bejoy Sing unable to oppose the Mahrattas any longer surrendered the fort and district of Ajmere to them in 1756. For thirty-one years, the Mahrattas held possession of Ajmere till 1787, when the Mahrattas were defeated in the battle of Tonga by the *Rahtores* and the Jeypore Raja. The Rahtores took possession of Ajmere but held it only for three years. But it was retaken then by De Boigne, the general of the Mahrattas, and was held by them till 1818, when by a treaty Dowlut Rao Sindia ceded the district of Ajmere to the British Government. Mr. Wilder, the first superintendent received charge of Ajmere from Bapa Sindia, the last Mahratta Subadar, on the 28th day of July, 1818. From this year the history of Ajmere is that of its administration by an Agent of the British Government. The

mutiny of 1857 passed like a cloud over the province.
There was no interruption at all of civil government. The
mutinous regiments marched direct to Delhi, and the
agricultural classes did not share in the revolt. Now
peace and prosperity reign supreme in Ajmere under the
beneficial rule of the British Government.

Marwara.

Little is known of the history of Marwara before
the annexation of Ajmere in 1818. Before that time it
was known as a hilly tract of land inhabited by an independent and plundering race. Maharaja Sewae Jey Sing of
Jeypore and Amir Khan of Tonk failed to chastise
the plunderers of Jak and Chang. Mr. Wilder the first
superintendent of Ajmere, entered into an agreement with
the owners of the villages of Marwara binding them to
abstain from plunder. But they dishonored the treaty
and went on as usual in their plundering excursions. In
1819, Mr. Wilder took without much difficulty the villages
one after another. In 1820, a general insurrection took
place. The thorough subjugation of the country was then
determined upon. A strong British Army retook Jak,
Lulna and Shamgarh, three of the villages of Marwara.
Borwa and Hatun were next attacked and taken. The
capture of Mundlan and Bursawara followed. Kot-Kirana
and Bagri in Marwar-Marwara were then taken and
made over to Jodhpur. The whole country submitted after
the capture of Ramgarh, the strongest of their forts, in
1821.

Captain Tod ruled over Meywar portion of it in the
name of the Rana, the Thakores governed the Marwar
portion of the territory and Mr. Wilder was superintend-

ent of Ajmere. But it soon appeared that this triple government of Ajmere-Meywar-Marwara was no government at all. There was no peace, nor any security of life and property in the land. Under these circumstances it was resolved that these portions should be brought under the management of one Officer.

Treatises were accordingly made with Oodeypore and Jodhpur; and Meywar-Marwara was annexed to Ajmere, and thenceforth came to be called Ajmere-Marwara. An English Officer governed the united territories ever since. This province and the whole of Rajpootana is now administered peacefully, wisely and prosperously by Colonel Walter, Agent, Governor-General, Rajpootana.

CHAPTER X.

Jhalawar.

Zalim Sing was the hereditary commander-in-chief of Kotah, who was nominated by its old chief as regent during the minority of his son, Oomed Sing. Zalim Sing exercised his power with extraordinary zeal and ability which induced Oomed Sing on attaining his majority to leave all authority in his hands. Raj Rana Zalim Sing became thus virtually the ruler of Kotah. After the death of Oomed Sing and Zalim Sing, dispute arose between their heirs for the throne of Kotah. They at last came to a compromise, whereby certain districts of the Kotah Raj were separated and ceded to the heirs of Zalim Sing, whereby the new State of Jhalawar was constituted in 1838, having for its capital, Jhalrapatan.

The chief of the State received the title of Maharaj Rana, was granted a salute of 15 guns and was placed on an equal footing with the other chiefs of Rajpootana.

Maharaj Rana Madan Sing was the first ruler of Jhalawar. He died in 1845 and was succeeded by his son, Prithi Sing, who rendered good service to the British Government during the Sepoy Mutiny, for which the Government tribute for the year 1857-58 was remitted. Prithi Sing had a good nature and happy disposition and was very popular with his subjects. In 1875, Prithi Sing died and was succeeded by his adopted son, Bakht Sing, the present chief. He was formally installed on the 24th June, 1876, on which he took the name of Zalim Sing. The Maharaj Rana of Jhalawar has not proved himself to be so good a ruler as he was expected to be when full governing powers were conferred upon him; and as misrule in the State was every-where brought to light, the administration of the State was placed in the hands of the Political Superintendent assisted by a Council. The finances of the State are in a sound condition, and suitable allowances have been made for the Maharaj Rana and his establishment. The Maharaj Rana of Jhalawar has been granted the right of adoption.

The revenue of Jhalawar is about Rupees 1,450,000.

CHAPTER XI.

Bundi.

Rao Dev who is said to have lineally descended from Agnipala the first Chohan, founded the city of Bundi in 1342. From the capital the State is named Bundi. He destroyed the *Minas* who occupied the Bundi valley and named the country Harawati or Harouti, so called from

F.

Ishtpal, his ancestor, who lived in 1025. A period of nearly two hundred years intervened from the reign of Rao Dev to that of Rao Surjan, throughout which period the *Haras* or the people of Harouti remained as quasi vassals of the Ranas of Oodeypore; but with the accession of Rao Surjan in 1533 a new era began. The famous fortress of Runthumbor had come into the possession of Rao Surjan by means of his relative Sawant Sing. The Emperor Akbar wanted to get it and obtained it by stratagem and courtesy, having failed to procure it by force of arms. Surjan Sing did good service to his Mogul lord and had Bemrao and Chunar added to his government. He built new edifices in Benares, and beautified and established perfect security to life and property throughout his dominions. He was succeeded by his son, Rao Bhoj, who like his father, did splendid services to Akbar, and was followed by his eldest son, Rao Rutton. He joined the imperial army at Burhanpur when Shah Jahan was threatening rebellion against his father, Jahangir.

Rao Rutton helped the emperor to defeat his rebellious son, Shah Jahan, and was rewarded with the government of Burhanpur. The Emperor bestowed in 1525 on his second son, Madhu Sing, the city of Kotah and its dependencies to be held by him and his heirs direct of the crown. Kotah and its dependencies belonged to the State of Bundi, and this gift of the Emperor divided Harouti into two parts to be ruled over by separate chiefs. Thus was Kotah separated for ever from Bundi. Rao Rutton was a good ruler and governed well and was respected and loved by his people. He was succeeded by his grandson, Chatter Sal, who was nominated by Shah Jahan, governor of the

Imperial capital, which post he held throughout his reign.
He also served under Aurungzebe in the Deccan and
remained faithful to Shah Jahan, and fought and died for
him at the battle of Dholpur in 1658, which gave the
empire to Aurungzebe. Chatter Sal was succeeded by his
son, Rao Bhao, who was threatened with ruin for the
sins of his father. He sent Atmaram to conquer Bundi
and annex it to the government of Runthumbor, but his
efforts proved unsuccessful. For the courage displayed
by the Haras, their Rao was forgiven and appointed
governor of Aurungabad. He erected here many beautiful
edifices and acquired much fame by his valour, his charity
and piety. He died in 1682 and was succeeded by Anurad
Rao, grandson of his brother Bhim. The new Rao served
under Aurungzebe in his wars in the Deccan and did
splendid services to the Emperor. Once he rescued the
Ladies of the *Seraglio* from the hands of the enemy and
distinguished himself in the seige and storm of Bejapore.
He died while engaged in settling the northern countries
of the Punjab and was succeeded by his son, Budh Sing.
He took up the cause of Bahadur Shah and assisted him in
gaining victory at the terrible battle of Jajao, in 1707.
For this signal service he received the title of Rao Raja
from the Emperor, and throughout his life fought in behalf of him, faithful to the tradition of his family. Budh
Sing met a new enemy in his brother-in-law, Jey Sing,
Raja of Jeypore, who deprived him of his patrimony, and
forced him to take refuge in Beygu where he died heart-
broken. His eldest son, Oomed Sing, after fourteen years'
struggle for the recovery of Bundi, at last regained possession of it in 1749. He lived a life of misfortune and misery
fifty-one years longer and died in 1804, after having abdi-

cated the throne to his son in 1771. His son died in his lifetime and was succeeded by his grandson, whose education and training he looked after for eight years till 1804. Bishan Sing, grandson of Oomed Sing, was an energetic and honest prince. He was also strong and brave and killed with his own hand more than one hundred lions and innumerable tigers and boars. He assisted the British Government in suppressing the Pindaries in 1817 and received as a reward many districts formerly seized by Holkar and Sindia. By the treaty of 1818, the British Government took Bundi under its protection. Bishan Sing was succeeded by his eldest son, Ram Sing, in 1821. He married a Princess of the Jodhpur family but treated her cruelly, for which war with that State would have taken place but for the timely interference of the British Government.

During the mutiny of 1857, the Maharao of Bundi showed himself indifferent to his allegiance to the Paramount Power contrary to the tradition of his family, and in consequence of which friendly intercourse with him was broken off by the British Government, and was not resumed till 1860. The Maharao Raja of Bundi is still hale and vigorous, notwithstanding his advanced age, and attends to every detail of the administration with the same watchful care that has always marked his rule. His eldest son is now, however, given some share of the work of the State, and takes an intelligent interest in its affairs. He has received the right of adoption and is entitled to a salute of 17 guns. The revenue of Bundi is about Rupees 500,000.

CHAPTER XII.

Bharatpur.

Churaman, a Jat landholder was the founder of the present ruling house in Bharatpur. He built two petty forts near Dig, from which he used to plunder the neighbouring country and even ventured to harass the army of the Emperor Aurungzebe. Jey Sing of Amber, who was sent against him by the Emperor, at first could not succeed in taking his little forts, but in 1712 assisted by Badan Sing, a younger brother of Churaman, he compelled Churaman to run away from his territory, and proclaimed Badan Sing as ruler of Dig with the title of Thakore. Thakore Badan Sing was succeeded by his son, Suruj Mul, who assumed the title of Raja and fixed his capital at Bharatpur. In 1754, he baffled the allied forces of Gazi-ud-din, the Mahrattas and the Raja of Jeypore. In 1760, he joined the Mahratta confideracy under Seodas Rao Bhao for the empire of India, but was lucky enough to sever his connection from it ere the fatal battle of Pannipat in 1761. He was strong enough to seize Agra. He was slain by a party of Beloochi horse while making an attempt on Delhi. He was succeeded by Jawaher Sing who again was followed by his brother, Ratan Sing. Kesri Sing, his infant son, succeeded him. Newal Sing, his uncle, ruled as Regent for Raja Kesri Sing. The Mahrattas having in 1768 recovered from the disastrous battle of Pannipat, reasserted their claim to tribute and invaded Bharatpur. The Regent bought them off with a large sum. Naval Sing was a man of great ability, but events were too strong for him. He died of dropsy in 1773 and was succeeded by Newal Sing as Regent. But his younger brother, the renowned Ranjit Sing, ambitious of power, sought the assistance of Najaf Khan, attacked and defeated his brother, the Regent, at Barsana, and took possession of Dig and finally of Bharatpur.

Ranjit Sing by the death of his nearer relations, became now the Raja of Bharatpur. Ranjit Sing was one of the Native Princes who desired to connect their interests with the British Government. With him a treaty was concluded at the beginning of the Mahratta war, guaranteeing the independent possession of his territories. He assisted Lord Lake in his campaign against Dowlut Rao Sindia and did good service at the battle of Laswari, for which the British Government rewarded him with the gift of five villages yielding seven lacs of rupees. He had acted as a friendly power to the British, till war was declared by the British Government against Holkar whom he secretly aided. When Holkar was defeated and his forces came to take shelter in Dig in 1804, the Raja's troops opened a destructive fire upon the pursuers. The army proceeded now to attack his forts. Dig was carried by assault in december 1804. Bharatpur was beseiged, in January 1805. This celebrated seige lasted for many months inflicting on the English great loss of money and men. The Raja well-defended the fort, but, seeing it was fruitless to quarrel with the British Lion he sent for peace, which was concluded on the 10th April, 1805. Raja Ranjit Sing, who gained in prestige and credit by repulsing the British troops from the Bharatpur walls, died in less than two years after his moral triumph. He was succeeded by his eldest son, Ranbir Sing, who furnished his contingent of troops to the British in the Pindari war, in 1817. He died in 1823 and was succeeded by his brother, Baldeo Sing, who in his turn, died in 1825. His infant son, Balwant Sing, succeeded him. But his cousin Durjan Sal dethroned him.

The British Gevernment interfered and a force of 25,000 men commanded by Lord Combermere, went and invested Bharatpur; and reduced the hitherto invulnerable mud fortress of Bharatpur in January, 1826; made Durjan Sal captive and installed Balwant Sing in February, 1826. In 1835, Raja Bulwant Sing assumed charge of his government and the political agency was withdrawn. The Raja died in 1853 and was succeeded by his only son, Jeswant Sing, the present ruler of Bharatpur, who is conducting the affairs of his Raj in a clever manner. The present chief of Bharatpur personally governs his State without a *Kamdar*, and takes a great interest in all that goes on in his territory. In December 1887, His Excellency the Ex-Viceroy, Lord Dufferin, visited Bharatpur and stayed there for a few days' shooting, and returned much pleased. The Maharaja Jeswant Sing Bahadur, G. C. S. I., has been granted the right of adoption and is entitled to a salute of seventeen guns.

The revenue of the State of Bharatpur is about Rupees 2,100,000.

CHAPTER XIII.

Karowlee.

The early history of this State is obscure. What is known of it dates from the decline of the Mogul Empire. The Raja of Karowlee is mentioned in the history of the Mahrattas as paying tribute to the Peshwa. Raja

Hurbuksh Pal ruled over the State when it was placed
under the protection of the Paramount British Power in
1817. The Raja showed discontented under British subjection and assisted a rebel prince; but at last he submitted
and was pardoned. He had some border differences with
Jeypore, but they were of little importance and were
easily settled. He died in 1838 and was succeeded by
Partap Pal, a son of his cousin, in default of a nearer heir.
One of the *Ranees* proclaimed herself pregnant, and, in
time, pretended to have delivered of a son. By appointing
a commission of enquiry, it was found out that the birth of
a son was untrue. Partap Pal was then formally recognized as Raja in 1839 and entered his capital in 1840 in
triumph. Throughout his reign, oppression, misgovernment
and out-breaks prevailed. He died childless and was succeeded by Narsing Pal, a minor relative, in 1848. A
political agent was appointed by the British Government
to control the factions and baffle intrigue. He died in
1852. Bharat Pal, a distant kinsman, adopted by him,
succeeded him. The Government of India intended to
annex it for misrule, but was prevented from doing so by
the interference of the House of Commons. It then recognized Bharat Pal as Raja of Karowlee. But it was soon
found out that there was a nearer relative who had higher
claims to the throne and whose cause was adopted by almost
all the *Ranees*, nobles and Jaghirdars.

The claims of Madan Pal the nearer relative were
admitted and he was placed on the throne in 1854. In
1857 during the Mutiny, Madan Pal did good service to
the British Government and he was richly rewarded. In
1859, a Political Agent was sent to assist the Maharaja in
clearing himself of debts. He was withdrawn in 1861.

Increased powers were given in June 18th, 1887, to the Maharaja of Karowlee, who uses them with discretion and in a manner calculated to benefit his State, which is now almost free from the burden of debt that has lain upon it for some years. The balance of debt is now about a lac which will be paid off by the next year.

Maharaja Madan Pal, the present ruler of Karowlee has been granted the right of adoption and is entitled to a salute of 17 guns.

The revenue of Karowlee is about Rupees 300,000.

CHAPTER XIV.

Tonk.

The principality of Tonk was founded by the famous free-booter, Amir Khan. He was born about 1751 in Rohilkand and was Afgan by birth. He first served in Malwa, then entered into the service of the Nawab of Bhopal. He then took service with the Rajpoot exchiefs of Raghugarh who supported themselves and their followers by plunder. Here he distinguished himself as a daring and fearless leader. In 1799 he threw his lot with Jeswant Rao Holkar and served under him as his immediate subordinate till 1806. Prior to 1806, Holkar had assigned to Amir Khan jaghirs in Malwa and Rajpootana forming the basis of the Principality of Tonk. The number of his followers gradually increased to 35,000 men, for whose support these jaghirs were found insufficient, and his lawless bands plundered Rajpootana, Malwa and Bundelkand. In 1807, Amir Khan entered the service of Jagat Sing, Maharaja of Jeypore, and assisted him in his contest with the Maharaja of Jodhpur for the hand of Kristna Kumari, the fair princess of Oodeypur. Jodhpur was hard pressed by Amir Khan, when he was led to change sides. Jeypore was then cruelly ravaged by Amir Khan. After having brought Rajpootana to the verge of ruin, Amir Khan proceeded in 1809 against the Mahratta family ruling in Nagore, over the throne of which he wished to plant his dynasty. But he was summoned away to his jaghirs by the demonstration of a British force against his own capital of Seronj. Having settled affairs in that quarter, he again fattened his followers on the spoils of Rajpootana and Malwa. He went on with his plundering excursions till 1817, when by a treaty with the British Government, Amir Khan was confirmed in the possession of the districts of Seronj, Pirawa, Gagal and Nimahera; and the British Government added to these as a free gift, the fort and district of Tonk-Rampura.

From this time Amir Khan gave up his predatory habits and engaged himself in settling his country, in building houses and palaces and in improving his territory. In the latter part of his life, he became pious and devout. He had twelve sons. He died in 1834 and was succeeded by his son, Wazir Mahamad Khan. This prince did good service during the Sepoy Mutiny, and, in reward, received the right of adoption. He died in 1864 and was succeeded by his son, Mahamad Ali Khan. The reign of this Nawah showed signs of tyranny in him. In 1865, he attempted to deprive the Lord of Lawa of his possessions and killed his prime minister and his attendants, and kept the Rajpoot Prince a close prisoner in the city of Tonk. But the British Government timely interfered and punished the Nawab by dethroning him and making Lawa a separate

Chiefship, and by reducing his salute from seventeen to eleven guns. Since Lawa has been created a separate State its condition is prosperous, and is daily improving under the able management of its lord.

Accordingly in 1868, the eldest son, Ibrahim Ali Khan, of the deposed Nawab, was placed upon the throne. This Prince is illiterate and extravagant. A council of regency was accordingly formed, presided over by a British officer to manage the affairs of government. This state of things lasted till a recent period when the Nawab got the management of the affairs of his State into his own hands. The condition of the State is being improved. The administration has now been established on a firm basis with a well-selected council and regular rules for the conduct of public business. The revenue survey and settlement under Captain Pears is making very satisfactory headway. The State debt has been reduced from 15½ lacs to 12½ lacs, and careful arrangements have been made for future reduction. A salute of seventeen guns is granted to the Nawab. His Highness is entitled to the right of adoption.

The revenue of Tonk is about Rupees 800,000.

CHAPTER XV.

Dholpur.

The founder of Dholpur State is Raja Dholun Deo Tuar, an offshoot of the family reigning at Delhi, who about A. D. 1005, resided at Belpur on the river Chambal ten miles southwest of the present town of Dholpur. Raja Dholun Deo built in the ravines of the river Chambal the old fort which exists up to date. The Karowlee Jadabs built Dholpur in 1120. The family of the ruling chief of Dholpur belongs to the *Deswati* tribe of Jats and is descended from Jeth Sing who settled at Bairat to the south of Ulwur in the eleventh century. He served under the *Tuar* Kings of Delhi, and after the fall of that Dynasty, one of his descendants settled on the lands of Bamroli where the family remained for one hundred and seventy-two years. Ruttan Pal Bamroli was driven out from Bamroli and settled in Gwalior. About 1490, Raja Man Sing of Gwalior succeeded in expelling the Mussulman governor from Dholpur and retained possession of it for several years; while the *Tuars* were driven from it by the Emperor Sekunder Lodi. Singun Deo, fifth in descent from Ruttan Pal, obtained in 1505 as a reward for great services done in an expedition into the Deccan, a formal grant from Raja Man Sing Tuar of Gwalior of the territory of Gohad, whence he assumed the title of Rana. Under Akbar, Dholpur and all the surrounding country belonged to the Subah of Agra, aad was ruled by Fateh-ul-lah and Mahabat Khan, after whom a new quarter of the city, Fateyabad, and an outlying suburb, Mahabatnagar, were called. In 1658, the battle for empire was fought at *Ranka Chobutra* near Dholpur between the sons of Shah Jahan. In 1782, Dholpur fell into the hands of Sindia. In 1803, it was occupied by the British, and at the end of the year it was ceded to Sindia again. In 1805, it was resumed by the English, who finally in 1806 uniting the purganas of Dholpur, Bari and Rajakhera with the *taluca* of *Sri* Muttra into one State, made it over to Maharaja Rana Kherut Sing, the ancestor of the present Rana of Dholpur, in exchange of his territory of Gohad. He died in 1836. The present ruler of the Dholpur State is Maharaj Rana Nehal Sing, a Jat of the *Bamralia* family, who was born in 1868 and is fourth in descent from Maharaj Rana Kherut Sing. The present ruler succeeded to the throne of Dholpur in 1873, on the death of his grand-father, Maharaj Rana Bhagwant Sing, his father having died in the life-time of his grand-father who did good service to the British Government in 1857 by rendering assistance to the British fugitives from Gwalior. The financial condition of this State has called for especial arrangements, loan and other, for the payment of the proportionately large amount of debt due by the State. This debt amounts now to over 15 lacs.

The Rana of Dholpur has got the right of adoption and is entitled to a salute of fifteen guns.

The revenue of Dholpur State is about Rupees 600,000.

CHAPTER XVI.

Banswara.

Jugmal, the younger son of Oodey Sing, ruler of Bagar, was the ancestor of the rulers of Banswara. He became its ruler in 1528. The sixth in descent from Jugmal was Samar Sing, who considerably extended his territory by conquest over the chief of Partapgarh. He was succeeded by his son, Kusal Singh, who fought for twelve years with the Bhils and founded Kusulgarh and other places in the province. In 1747, Prithi Sing came into power. He fortified the town of Banswara and seized the district of Chilkari. Towards the end of the 18th century, the Mahrattas overran the country, plundered and levied heavy exactions. The Rawal Oomed Sing applied for British protection, which was extended to him in 1818 by a treaty.

G.

The Bhils continued to disturb the State. Oomed Sing was succeeded by his son, Bhawani Sing, who again was succeeded by Bahadur Sing, one of the nobles of the State. Bahadur Sing died without issue and was succeeded by Luchman Sing, the present ruler. The State of Banswara is much embarrassed financially and has therefore been placed under the close supervision of a special Political officer.

The Rawal of Banswara has been granted the right of adoption and is entitled to a salute of fifteen guns.

The revenue of Banswara is about Rupees 3,00,000.

CHAPTER XVII.

Partapgarh.

The Partapgar family is descended from Khim Sing, second son of Rana Mokul and younger brother of Rana Kumbhu of Oodeypur. Suruj Mull, son of Khim Sing, for contesting the throne of Meywar, was driven out from it. Bhag Sing succeeded Suruj Mull and sacrificed his life for safety of Oodey Sing, the infant son of Rana Sanga. Bhag Sing was succeeded by his son, Rai Sing, and it was his son, Bhika, who founded the town of Deogarh or Deolia in 1561. Tej Sing succeeded his father Bhika, in 1579, who again was succeeded by Bhano in 1594. Bhano was killed in 1594 fighting against Jodh Sing of Meywar at Jiran, and was succeeded by Singho, who again was succeeded by his eldest son, Jeswant Sing, in 1623. Jeswant Sing and his eldest son, Mah Sing, and all his followers were killed by Jagat Sing of Oodeypore, and a Meywar force was located in Deolia. Hari Sing, second Son of Jeswant Sing, through the interest of Mahabat Khan and his own address and feats of strength, obtained from the Emperor Shah Jahan a grant of the district of Kanthal, the local name for Partapgarh. He drove away the Meywar force and established himself as Maharaja at Deolia, built a palace and enlarged his territory by the conquest of the district lying north-east of Partapgarh. Hari Sing was succeeded in 1674 by his eldest son, Partap Sing, who founded Partapgarh, the present capital of the State. Prithi Sing succeeded his father, Partap Sing, in 1708 and he, in his turn, was succeeded by his grandson, Ram Sing, in 1717. Oomed Sing succeeded his nephew, Ram Sing, who was succeeded in 1723 by his brother, Gopal Sing. Nothing important happened in this reign also. He died in 1758 and was succeeded by Salim Sing, who proceeded to Delhi and obtained permission to coin money in his name, called *Salim Shahi* rupee. He was succeeded by Sawant Sing, during whose reign the Mahrattas overran the whole country. Sawant Sing became tributary to Holkar. The State of Partapgarh was taken under British protection in 1818. Sawant Sing ruled for sixty-nine years. He died in 1844 and was succeeded by Dulpat Sing, the second grandson of Raja Sawant Sing, who had been adopted in 1825 as Raja of Dungarpur, his son, Dip Sing, and his first grandson, Kesri Sing, having died before him.

Dulpat Sing adopted Oodey Sing as his successor in Dungarpur and renounced his connection with it. He died in 1864 and was succeeded by his son, Oodey Sing, the present ruler of Partapgarh.

Raja Oodey Sing has been granted the right of adoption and is entitled to a salute of fifteen guns.

The revenue of the State of Partapgarh is about Rupees 2,62,400.

CHAPTER XVIII.

Dungarpur.

The ruling chief of Dungarpur is descended from an elder branch of the family that now rules in Oodeypore. He belongs to the *Sesodia* clan of Rajpoots and has the title of Maharawal. About the beginning of the 15th century a descendant of the elder brother of the Rana of Oodeypore conquered the country of the *Bhils* and became the ruler of the province of Bagar, made up of Banswara and Dungarpur. Oodey Sing who came to rule it in 1509, fought under Rana Sanga against Babar in 1527 at *Kanua* and was killed. He had two sons, Prithi Raj and Jugmal, the elder became the founder of the Dungarpur family and the younger that of Banswara. Dungarpur remained subject to the Mogul Emperors and paid them tribute, and then became tributary to the Mahrattas. Subsequently the State became a prey to the Pindaries and other free-booters. At last in 1818, it was taken under British protection. During the administration of Rawal Jeswant Sing, great disorders prevailed in the land caused by the discontented Thakores assisted by the Bhils, when a British force was sent to bring them into order.

Jeswant Sing was an incompetent ruler and was there-fore deposed in 1825; and his adopted son, Dalpat Sing, the younger grandson of Raja Sawant Sing of Partapgarh, succeeded him. In 1844, Dalpat Sing gained the *gaudi* of Partapgarh and was permitted to adopt Oodey Sing as his successor in Dungarpur. But he ruled both the States till 1852, as the Maharaja of Partapgarh and as Regent of

Dungarpur. But the double government did not prove successful. He therefore resigned all power in Dungarpur which was put under a native agent till Rawal Oodey Sing, the present chief of Dungarpur, attained his majority. He has now assumed the administration of the State.

He has got the right of adoption and is entitled to a salute of 15 guns.

The revenue of Dungarpur is about Rupees 75,000.

CHAPTER XIX.

Kishengarh.

Kishen, the ninth son of Oodey Sing, Raja of Jodhpur, was the founder of the Kishengarh State. It was founded in 1613, and is situated in a spot beyond the limits of Marwar. Permission to found a new state was given to him by the Emperor Shah Jahan, as a reward for his having murdered his uncle Guj Sing of Jodhpur. The history of this State up to 1790 has nothing to record. The inhabitants of this State are mainly *Jats*. The government was and is patriarchal. It being a very small State, its ruler could not take any prominent part in the many struggles that characterised the 18th century. It is infertile and has not for a long time to pay any tribute to the Moguls and to the Mahrattas. Bahadur Sing, chief of Kishengarh, unpatriotically assisted the Mahrattas in gaining victories over the united forces of Jodhpur and Jeypore at the battle of Patan and Mairta in 1790 and 1791 respectively. The last great battle brought the whole of Rajpootana except Kishengarh under the subjection of the Mahrattas. Bahadur Shah was succeeded by Kalyan Sing who placed his little State under British protection in 1818 under a treaty with usual conditions.

Shortly after the conclusion of the treaty, the Raja began to act as a man having insanity and no principle and mis-managed the affairs of government. A civil commotion took place and many of the nobles revolted against him. Actual hostilities commenced between the rival parties. The British Government drew the attention of the Raja to these disordered state of things in his State and informed him that he should be held answerable for it. The Raja marched against his rebellious barons, but his adherents left him at the time of action. He fled to Ajmere and appealed to the British Government for aid. The disaffected nobles declared their intention to depose Kalyan Sing, and proclaimed his infant son as the Ruler of the State and invoked British arbitration. The British Government informed the Raja that they intended to have the State managed by a Regency to which the Raja did not consent. Finally all civil strife was brought to a close by Kalyán Sing having retired from Kishengarh and abdicated the throne in favour of his son. He died in 1839 and was succeeded by his son, Prithi Sing, the present chief of Kishengarh. Steady progress is found every where. Changes have been introduced in the system of accounts and the administration of justice. Irrigation-works are under construction, and attention is paid to better methods of agriculture. Differences between the Maharaja and his chief feudatory, the Raja of Futteygarh, are in process of adjustment.

The Maharaja of Kishengarh has got the right of adoption and is entitled to a salute of fifteen guns.

The revenue of Kishengarh is about Rupees 6,00,000.

Finis.

NOTICE.

WORKS BY BABOO AMRITA LAL DE, B. A., B. L., PROFESSOR OF HISTORY,

MAHARAJA'S COLLEGE,

Jeypore, Rajpootana.

		Price.		Postage
		Rs.	Ans.	Ans.
1.	Theosophy	,,	4	1
2.	Kissa San Eli or Urdoo Translation of Gulliver's Travel to Lilliput ...	,,	8	1
3.	Key to the Companion Reader ...	1	,,	2
4.	The Flowers of India ...	1	8	2
5.	An Essay on Cow-slaughter ...	,,	8	1
6.	The Students' History of Rajpootana	1	,,	2

Apply with
remittances
to the *author.*